TREES IN GOD'S GARDEN

Through Channel Laurel Steinhice

The Gospel of Thomas Interviews By
LISA HANES

lightsourcegroup.com

lightsourcegroup.com

Acknowledgements

The channel and interviewer gratefully thank the St. Thomas Christian Church for their generous sharing of the translated passages from the Gospel of Thomas. All the passages from the Gospel of Thomas that appear in this book are taken from the St. Thomas Christian Church translation used in their study programs.

For additional information about the St. Thomas Christian Church, please contact:

Shirley Chambers
Karin Kabalah Center
2531 Briarcliff Road
Atlanta, Georgia 30329
404.320.1038
kabalah@mindspring.com

INTRODUCTION

October 28, 2009

It wasn't planned, really…it sort of just happened. My friend Laurel Steinhice, a powerful voice and energy channel, and I had done hundreds of channeling sessions over the past 20 years. We had talked with Edgar Cayce about healing and world events. We had talked with the Arch Angels Michael, Azariel, and Raziel about human development and history. We had spoken with off-planet entities on topics like planetary development and the role of earth in the universal scheme. We had grand conversations with Ben Franklin who, by the way, is very entertaining and still passionate about American politics! We had even talked with Isa – Jesus – on many occasions about a whole range of topics.

Through all these years and channeling sessions, we didn't have the intent to share our conversations with the Guides. Many were, in fact, private sessions of mine that had to do with personal growth and often included my struggles to understand age old questions like, "Who am I?" and "What am I doing here?" You know, those simple questions.

It wasn't until Laurel enrolled in a study program with the St. Thomas Christian Church that the idea for a book began to take shape. Part of her studies included reading a variety of books that covered key concepts in spiritual teaching and modern philosophy. Laurel began to pass on to me those books she thought I would find particularly interesting.

One book was *The Gospel of Thomas: The Hidden Sayings of Jesus*, by Marvin Meyer (HarperCollins, 1992). Frankly, before reading the book, I was not familiar with the text known as the Gospel of Thomas. Unlike the other gospels found in the King James version of The Bible (just so we're clear on which *version* of Bible we're talking about), the Gospel of Thomas is a collection of Jesus' teachings rather than a chronological story of his life.

The Gospel of Thomas, along with other ancient texts, was found in Nag Hamadi, Egypt in 1948. *The Gospel of Thomas: The Hidden Sayings of Jesus* book includes all 114 passages in the original Coptic text on one side and an English translation on the other side.

As I read the passages, I was increasingly challenged to understand their meaning. After all, there are thousands of years of changing societal structure and several languages between the writing of the original text and my reading. Suddenly, I found myself *yearning* to be able to sit on a park bench somewhere with Jesus at my side and talk with him about his teachings.

Then there came the moment when I slapped myself on the forehead and said, "I can do that!" While we wouldn't use a park bench, my living room or Laurel's living room would work just fine.

Almost immediately after that realization, I began wondering how many others at some point in their lives have had that same yearning. What if *you* could sit down with Jesus and talk with him for hours or days? What would you ask? What would you want to know?

While I couldn't ask questions for everyone, I could use the Gospel of Thomas passages as a starting point for a book and hope that Jesus' answers would cover some relevant subjects for readers. Some subjects? Boy, was I in for a surprise!

Laurel and I spent about two months recording sessions with Jesus. We covered each passage with me reading the English translation and him explaining the meaning in the words. Once we had covered all 114 passages, it was time to begin transcribing the session tapes.

Over the next three months I became almost totally immersed in the transcription work. I spent days at a time working on the transcriptions without being involved in much else other than eating and sleeping. It filled my every waking moment and almost every thought.

I would hear something on the radio and think, "Jesus talked about that in passage 42!" A friend would talk about a problem or concern and I'd say to myself, "He covered that in passage 89!" I'd hear about a world event and think, "That relates to passage 77!" For about three months, everything I heard or thought about had a relationship to something Jesus said from the passages. It was amazing to realize how completely he had covered subjects that everyone could understand and apply to their own lives.

So, with all that said, how should you read this book? The best answer is, of course, any way you want to. Some people have read it cover to cover, front to back. Others have read one passage a day. Still others have picked it up and opened it to a passage at random. Ever do that with a book? Ask for help with a particular issue and open it to a page at random? It's amazing how well the content on that page will relate to your question!

In any event, I hope you read *Trees in God's Garden* with an open heart and mind. You can find truth in many places. It doesn't really matter if it's channeled through a person's voice, spray painted on a wall, or drawn in a Peanuts cartoon. The more unlimited our vision, the more unlimited our spirit and we can open to the Light within.

You know, I'll bet Jesus talks about that somewhere in the book, too!

Enjoy.

Lisa Hanes
Interviewer and Editor

8

Prologue by Jesus

When I walked the earth, I was called Isa. Now, many people call me Jesus, or the Christ. I became the Christ, the anointed, resurrected Holy One, by virtue of my death and resurrection. When I walked the earth as a man, I was the Word made flesh, the Light of God made manifest in a body that was truly human, born of a human woman, to experience humanity. As I learned and grew, I came to feel, more and more, what the ordinary human felt. Yet, in my earthly experience, never did I lose the sense of who I am – the Light of God.

When I came of age and was initiated by ritual baptism by my teacher and friend, John the Baptist, I began what the churches now call my ministry. I began to minister unto the people as a teacher and a healer. Every teacher is challenged from time to time to find the best way of saying what you want the student to receive and understand. Every teacher is challenged to put into 'user friendly' words, that what he chooses to teach. Never was this more true of any teacher, more so than of myself.

What I came to teach was far above what the ordinary, average human had any background for…beyond the rudimentary spiritual vibration. And, it was also above and beyond what even the most intellectual and learned scholars knew of how the universe works. It was vibrationally beyond anything humanity had ever encountered before, since that initial moment of receiving the breath of life – Adam, if you will, receiving the breath of life from God.

So, I was challenged to give my teaching in a way the human could receive it. I told stories. I used parables. I used comparisons and metaphors. People would say,

"What is the kingdom of heaven like?" And, I would say, "Well, it's like this…" or "It's like that…" and tell, perhaps, a different story each time. And, just like some of your political figures today who have one speech they give over and over on the campaign trail, when I found a story that worked, I had a tendency to use it over and over again! I developed this little stock of stories that I used as teaching tools, to reach the hearts and minds of those who heard with their ears, and who heard with their hearts.

Many times, I knew that what I was saying or doing would be incomprehensible to the greater number of persons present, and that I was speaking to a small percentage of a larger audience. And, then I would say, "He who has eyes, let him see. He who has ears, let him hear." Meaning, yes, I'm talking to you! If you can hear this, I'm talking to you. If you can see this, I'm showing this to you. Don't worry about the fact that the others can't see it or hear it. They will find it in their own time.

As my ministry began, I attracted a group of companions who had been specially prepared, by being born at the right time in the right place, so that they might have the opportunity to choose – and, yes, they had the right to choose – whether or not to be my friends, my companions, and my followers. They called me 'Master,' for I was their teacher. And, I called them my students or my disciples.

Among them were twelve who became, along with certain others who sometimes went with us, sort of a traveling entourage, just as…oh, I believe it's called 'roadies' today in entertainment groups! They were my roadies and my backup singers and my band, and I was the lead singer, as it were, and yet, we were a band of companions. Each one had the opportunity to express himself freely, whether he agreed with me or not. Each one had the opportunity to show his or her talents – for, of course, there were some women who were a part of our inner circle – and each one had the opportunity to learn and grow by experience, as well as by education. I gave them lectures, if you will, but by just being on the road with me, it was rather like the lab part of the class. They had the chance to see how people reacted to me. They had the chance to form their own opinions and learn from observations.

Just standing next to me was a change in vibration, for as I took them into my companionship, into my heart as friends and brothers, my aura grew to encompass them, and we were as One. As you well know, the vibration of sharing in a spiritual family auric exchange is in and of itself an exultation, a joy, and a delight, and I guess if there hadn't been anything else on my mind, we could just have sat around and grooved on each other's energy, endlessly! Actually, that's sort of what nirvana is like – just enjoying the sharing of the group energy, the universal energy of All That Is.

In any case, I did have a bit more of an agenda than just grooving on the energy together. And, as my teachings became more complex, they became more and more challenging to the powers that be – the governmental powers that be, the Romans, and the religious powers that be, the priests and scribes, the Pharisees, the counselors and so forth. The more these powers saw of me, the more uncomfortable it made them. Some of them were touched and shamed by the sudden understanding that I was teaching what *they* should have been teaching all along. Some of them felt the raw power of my Godhood and were afraid of it. And, they looked for a moment in which I slept, or was otherwise unwary, so they might strike me down in a moment of weakness, and go back to feeling comfortable again. For, the mere presence of my power did, in fact, make them uncomfortable. As you know,

Light has a tendency to shine into the dark corners and call to one's attention things that the individual might rather have swept under the rug, or left to an infinity of tomorrows to deal with.

So, knowing where it would lead, for I did know where it would lead, I was very much aware during much of my teaching that I wouldn't be there to keep the teaching going indefinitely. The time would come when my companions, my disciples, would receive the mantle of mastery. They would be the teachers and the healers, and the Light vested in me having been shared with them through my presence, through my words, and by my Godly choice, that Light would live in them, and they would have the power to pass it on to others. Again and again, I said, "Everything I have done, this you will do and more."

I knew I wouldn't be there in a human body to walk beside them, my sandals in the dust. And, yet, I would be there with them, always, to walk beside them in their hearts and minds, and in the energy that remembering me called forth in them.

All of them had the ability to call forth within themselves my own true Light, for I chose to share it with them. Each of them had the ability to speak my words, for I shared my words and thoughts with each of them. Yet, each of them had, as I did when I walked the earth – for that matter, as I always do – free will. And, if he spoke my words in a way that didn't feel quite right to him, he changed a little bit here and there to suit himself.

It is a curious thing that some disciples had more clarity on one subject than on others. If you ask me who best exemplified my words and thoughts by his teaching, I would have to say it was John for this, and James for that, and Paul for this, and Peter for that. But, Thomas, he took a bit of a different approach. He chose to record his personal memories of my teachings rather than give an historical account of my life.

Perhaps that is partly because we sat down together after my death and resurrection, and he said, "You have asked us to teach as you taught, and to heal as you healed, and I am quite prepared, I am committed to going forth into the world to teach and to heal in your name. Tell me, how can I do that best?" And, I said, "Follow your own heart, for my words are already written there." I am touched, even now, by the deep bond of that moment. I said, "Don't ever be afraid to reach for the power of healing, for I will never withhold it from you." Those were the only two specific instructions I gave him.

It is true that the Gospel of Thomas, as it is now called, was written by someone who heard it from Thomas some years after my death. It was copied from what Thomas wrote, and it was copied from what Thomas said that other people wrote down. So, the sayings, the questions, the answers – even the simplest of them – have passed through many hands before it has come to this. Now, having said all that, the Gospel of Thomas, as it is found in its present imperfections, has passed through far fewer hands than the other gospels and the other New Testament material, for they have been translated, retranslated, mythologized, and trod upon as it were, heavily, by many generations of scholars – well meant and otherwise. So, even imperfect as it is, the Thomas material is the closest to the original.

I have enjoyed this project that has allowed me to remember, to clarify, to interpret, and to comment on some of the teachings, and the little stories I used to tell when I walked the earth before I became the resurrected Christ. It brings me great joy to find an audience.

You know, when I stood on the hill and spoke to the people who gathered below me, I showed my true self to them, I showed my Light, and I spoke to each one who had ears to hear. I showed myself, my true self, to each and every one who had eyes to see. And, this I do now through this book. I speak to each one who has ears to hear, and I reveal myself to each one who has eyes to see. It is your choice, as a reader, to hear, or not to hear. To see, or not to see. To be stimulated by it, or to be bored by it. It is your choice to receive it, or not to receive it.

I welcome you, the reader, into my Light, just as I welcomed the multitudes back when I was your brother Jesus, a man – and a God – who walked the earth.

Passage 1

Jesus said: He who uncovers the significance of these words shall not taste death.

He who knows the full truth and significance of these words will have opened within his own being the gates of his own divinity. And he will not taste the bitterness of death, the lack of understanding of transition from one state of being to another. Whether he ascends or whether he chooses the death crossing, he will not taste the bitterness of death for he will know it is but new life in its seedling form. He, who understands my words and knows the significance of what I came to teach and the way I came to show, will not taste of death, though he may briefly go through its doors. He will know it is but a small thing; just a little speed bump on the road of life. No more than this, for the long road of life stretches far.

The key word here is bitterness, to regret death. The word bitter does not appear in this verse and yet that is what I meant and actually what I said at the time. I said, "He who understands my words, will never experience the bitter taste of death." And it is still true today. The bitterness of death has much to do with looking backward and having regrets. Guilt and regrets are always about the past. Fears and anxieties are about the future. And the Now stands in the moment between the two. The Now can be, by personal growth, spiritual awakening and personal choice, unencumbered by either the past or the future. The eternal moment experienced in joy.

Someone who allows his own inner-tuition, inner

knowing, to join with the teaching I have brought and finds this union of inner knowing and external God Light, will never taste a bitter death. Even if there is death, it will be a sweet one.

Passage 2

Jesus said, "The one who seeks must not cease seeking until he finds, and when he finds, he shall be troubled, and if he is troubled, he will marvel, and he will rule over the All."

The one who seeks must not cease seeking. You can't stop once your feet are truly well and goodly on the path. You know this. And by seeking, I do not mean simply playing around with it, but to allow that desire within to put you in the right direction that says, "I want to know…I want to understand." He who seeks must not stop seeking. For, if he abruptly truncated his journey, it would have an emotionally devastating impact on him. You and other seekers know that is a true thing. But, when I said it, a great many people didn't know that to stop the seeking would be expensive. So, I said, he who seeks must not cease seeking. And I was saying to them, don't take on the commitment of being a seeker with the idea that you can give it up somewhere along the way and not be touched by it. He who seeks must continue to seek.

When he finds, he will be troubled. When you find a truth you have long sought for, it has a disconcerting tendency to upend and tumble your life. Old illusions fall away. And, then, there is a time of evaluation. To trouble is to stir or disturb – think of troubling the waters. It is to stir the waters, to put movement into them instead of letting them lie there, stagnant. The flowing stream is troubled whereas the stagnant pond is not. So, when you seek, you become like the flowing stream: troubled from time to time by the upheaval that new ideas bring into your life. The upheaval that movement brings. That change brings. It's the eternal adventure.

He who is troubled will marvel. He who is troubled and begins to look upon his own beliefs and experiences with new eyes of understanding will see what has not before been revealed to him. And, will he not marvel at what he sees? He will say, "Was this here all along and I didn't know it? I didn't see it?" Discovery is a great joy, and that, too, is part of the eternal adventure.

He who seeks can't stop without paying a heavy price. He who seeks and finds will experience the troubling of the placid pool of his old beliefs. He who endures and goes with the flow of the troubling of this placid pool will marvel at what he finds. And, now the question: What does he find?

Himself. He finds his own divinity, alongside his own humanity. And, then, he knows the supreme, sublime oneness of being joined in consciousness to All That Is. It is nirvana. At that point he knows the God self and rules the All. For, when this bit of human consciousness has truly sought and endured the troubling, and continued to seek and marvel for as long as it takes, when at last he stands stripped to the core, all illusions gone, and beholds the God within, then he will have become one with God. Wise and worthy of co-creatorship. And not just able, but worthy of his own Godhood. And, he will see no separation between himself and the All.

Passage 3

Jesus said, "If the ones who lead you say, 'There is the kingdom, in heaven,' then the birds will go first before you into heaven. If they say to you, 'It is in the sea,' then the fish shall go before you. Rather, the kingdom is within you and outside you. If you know yourselves, then you will be known and you will know that you are sons of the living Father. But if you do not know yourselves, then you are in poverty, and you are poverty."

This has to do with saying the kingdom of heaven is not a place; it is a condition. I said if someone tells you the kingdom of heaven is there in the sky, then clearly the birds are closer to it than you are. And, if everybody takes off on his or her way to heaven, the birds are going to get there first. If I say to you the kingdom of heaven is in the sea, geographically in a fixed location, then clearly the fish and the other creatures of the sea are closer to it than you are. And, if we all take off for heaven, they're going to get there before you do.

But, the kingdom of heaven is not in a place, so that some creatures are geographically closer to it than others. It is within you and it is all around you. You know, I like the way they said it in the movie *Star Wars*. It is the Force. It is the life-stuff of the universe. It is within you – you are made of it. And, it is all around you. In the Vedic traditions it is called 'explicit manifest brahman.' That is, the life stuff, brahman, of the universe that has been made explicit – it has been explained by creative intent – and therefore has been made manifest into a maya that is very tangible-seeming.

This is what you are made of, explicit manifest brahman. You are the energy, the life force God has shaped into a beginning and a flow. And, a continued flow and a continued evolution. The point that it is evolutionary doesn't change the fact that it was God's idea! I'm speaking here of physical evolution as well as spiritual evolution.

The 'unmanifest implicit brahman' is that life force, that energy which has not yet been shaped creatively into maya or tangible seeming illusion. It is the raw material. It surrounds us all. Us as well as you. We are all within it. We are all it. And, there's plenty more where that came from – endlessly. It is unlimited.

So, if you think you have no more options, if you think you are in poverty, with no energy to draw on, then your belief makes it so. And, you have created poverty and you have become what you have created. But, if you know the kingdom of heaven is within you, how could you ever be impoverished in the ways that count? Oh, yes, you might undergo hardships, not realizing at the moment that somehow your particular higher self choice process has placed you on this portion of the hard path, but you can never truly be poor, for you are rich in life.

You are life. You are co-creator force – life force – and there is plenty more of this life stuff that you can draw on to manifest.

So, you see, that passage all has to do with saying "Shambahala," "paradise," the "Elysian fields," the glorious afterworld is not a place. It is a condition and its place is within you. And, yes, I would say so is hell. It's not a place; it's a condition of being separated from God's Light.

Passage 4

Jesus said, "The man old in his days will not hesitate to ask a baby of seven days about the place of life, and he will live. For many who are first shall be last, and they shall become a single one."

The elder is wise enough to know – if he is a wise elder – that the seven day old baby has come from a place of close proximity to God's Light, and will not hesitate to look upon this child with wonder and to say, "Little one, what have you come to teach me? What light have you come to bring?" And, woe to those who do not see the Light in the child, whatever their ages.

The wise man does not hesitate to receive teaching from a young one. And, he will live because of his wisdom and his ability to receive the light from any teacher and any vessel of Light that God may put in his path. Those who are so filled with the vanity of their own importance – who are so intent on being right that they are not willing to see wisdom anywhere other than within themselves – become crystallized within this high order of illusion. Those who can only see wisdom (or if you prefer the term, 'learning opportunity') in the limited narrow strictures of clear, short-term self-advantage are dying by their own hands and by their own hearts. By the closed nature of their minds and hearts, they create the swiftly growing seeds of their own death.

The child, by the very nature of his beginning, generally carries more of God's own Light than the adult. And, it is a wise elder who does not hesitate to acknowledge this and learn from it. When the elder looks at the little babe and sees God's Light in the child, he is acknowledging his own divinity and wisdom as well as the child's. And, he will live. He will live – and this is a particularly Jewish belief and tradition – he will live in his children, and in his children's children, and in their children beyond him, for the generations that flow from your life are your gift of life to life.

The child in the arms of the parent receives the aura of the parent as nourishment – and infants who do not have this will sicken and die. And, the parent with the child in her arms also receives the pure nourishing essence of the child's energy, and it is a strengthening and a great lesson. So, this old fellow of whom I spoke was wise indeed, and his wisdom and his Light will live forever, for it is a part of All.

We are all expressions of the one everlasting, complex, amalgamation that people tend to call God. All of us together are the single One.

Passage 5

Jesus said, "Know what is in front of your face, and what is concealed from you will be revealed to you. For there is nothing concealed which will not be manifest."

It's as plain as the nose on your face. When people keep trying to look beyond the obvious without first having understood the obvious, it is an exercise in folly. Know what is in front of your face. Well, maybe it's a rock. How are you going to learn what's on the other side of the rock unless you say, "Oh, there's a rock in front of me," and acknowledge the rock. Even if you use your psychic gifts to see beyond the rock, you have to acknowledge there's a rock!

Know what is in front of your face. If there's an obstacle in your path, recognize there's an obstacle. If there is a resource in your hand, recognize that it is a resource. Don't go looking for more distant things while ignoring what's around you. I have been saying recently through this channel, "Learn to live from the inside out." Recognize the Light within you. Your own Light is in your face. Know it and then when you know it, you claim it and own it and begin to let it grow, and everything else is revealed to you one layer at a time.

I go back to the Kabalistic teaching – for I knew Kabalah when I was incarnate as Jesus. Kabalah explains the word nature as 'one's essential purpose.' It is the nature of the fire to burn. It is the nature of water to flow, and to be wet. It is the nature of the tree to grow and leaf out. Everything has an essential nature.

It is the nature of God to create. It is the nature of God to love. All that you are experiencing now, the layers upon layers of mystery as they are peeled back exposing the next layer, is a product of God's nature to create. You create the layers as you peel them off. The peeling process itself is also creation. You want it to be deeper? Your creative power makes it deeper. You want it more detailed and complex? Your creative power makes it so.

Even as we speak about this passage we are creating new layers of meaning. The seed of me in my intended message was sown in those words when I first spoke them. And although those seeds were nourished and allowed to sprout and were brought forth to the 2000 year period, still now, they are bearing new fruit. And they are evolving along with humanity's ability to perceive more and deeper meaning.

Passage 6

His disciples asked him: "Do you want us to fast, and how shall we pray, and shall we give alms, and what food regulations shall we keep?" Jesus said, "Do not lie, and do not do what you hate, because all is revealed before heaven. For nothing is hidden that shall not be revealed, and nothing is covered that shall remain without being revealed."

    The disciples were asking, "What rules do you want us to follow in order to keep faith with you and stay with the instructions you've given us?" And, I was really quite annoyed because I knew they didn't get the message. And I said to them, "It's not about following rules. It's not about rituals."

    Don't do work you hate. It's not true to yourself to keep doing it. You may not hate it so very much if it is only a stepping-stone that takes you where you want to go. But, there is no more soul crushing, spirit ripping thing than to keep on doing work you hate.

    Don't lie; you can't hide it. If you think giving up pleasures and fasting, and going to church, and keeping dietary laws is going to get you into the higher vibrational realms of paradise, you are mistaken. Those are cheap tickets to way stations where you'll have to learn more. Fasting, giving alms, if it is done just to try to buy the cheap ticket, is of no value. If you want to fast, it should be because you want to. Usually for a vision quest. To make a point. To prove to yourself that you have discipline. But, it should be what you want, or don't do it.

Giving alms should not be to show off and say, "I have lots of money and I can afford to give it." It should not even be, "I had better do this because someday somebody may show mercy on me." Even that is not enough. It should be because you see someone and your heart goes out to him or her and you may say as you give, "I wish I had more to give, but I will share with you what I have."

You may even think to yourself it is appropriate that I give this much and not ten times that amount. For, if I gave ten times that amount, it would unbalance the receiver's pattern and life choices. I will give what he can receive. Enough that he may feel his stress diminish. Enough that he may rejoice. But, not enough that his life may be overturned. Give from the joy of your heart, not because someone said you are supposed to. Not because you think it will earn you brownie points with God. Give because it is your choice to give.

Service should not be sacrifice. It should be joy.

And, if you think God doesn't know the difference, then read that verse again, for nothing is concealed from spirit, from perception. You can't pretend to be a cheerful giver. You have to *be* a cheerful giver to earn that title. You can't pretend to be a joyful giver. It has to be joyful, otherwise, don't bother to do it. Pretending is a very self-serving illusion that attempts to buy favor with God – or with your community.

The part about all being known – well, you know this is so, if for no other reason, that you live in the information age. How hard it is to keep a secret from the government or from the paparazzi these days, much less from God! God sees even the government's secrets and those of the paparazzi! There's a fine line between cherishing one's inner privacy and trying to hide something. Privacy is something that is between you and God, and you and God can work it out together and be comfortable about it together. But, don't try to lie to God. It doesn't work. You are only lying to yourself. Shakespeare said it later, "This above all, to thine own self be true."

Passage 7

Jesus said, "Blessed is the lion which the man shall eat, and the lion will become man; and cursed is the man whom the lion shall eat, and the lion will become man."

The lower vibrational creature tends to benefit from the energy of an exchange. And the higher vibrational creature, if he is consumed by a lower vibrational one, loses ground. The lion who is consumed, or who is taken in by the man is blessed by connection to the higher energy. But, the man who is taken in by the lion has lost something. The word 'eat' in this passage doesn't mean eat like food, and it doesn't mean to kill either. Eating in this sense meant ingested, digested, but in another way.

You see, even if you take the word eat literally, there was a ritual eating of the heart of the enemy or certain body parts of the enemy. There was ritual cannibalism, which is not the same thing as hunger cannibalism. When primitive tribesmen ate the heart of the lion to gain a lion's courage, the lion was ennobled. The same primitive tribesmen who would eat the heart of a lion would often also eat the heart of a human if they killed him, and he was strong enough. It is an animal behavior.

For the human to be dominant is really what it's all about. When the human is dominant, when the higher vibrational being is dominant, it helps to raise the vibration of the non-dominant.

If I take you into myself, wouldn't you be raised in vibration? But, if I lost myself in you, I would be lowered and you would be raised. Read it again. Either way, the lion gets raised.

Higher energy lifts up lower energy. If higher energy dominates, it does not diminish and the lower energy is lifted up. If the lower energy dominates, the lower energy is still lifted up, but the higher energy is diminished. That means there is a natural order of hierarchy in which higher vibration always gives – always – by association to the lower. But, whether the higher energy maintains itself or is diminished, depends on whether it – man in this case – has maintained its dominance or has been lowered by defeat, and was consumed by the lower energy.

Now, think of this allegorically in a sexual context. You know very well that when a higher vibrational being is intimate with someone of lower vibration, there is a tendency for the person of lower vibration to be raised by association with a higher vibration aura. So long as the higher vibrational person is dominant in the relationship, this is not necessarily a 'fall.' But, if the person whose vibration is higher is dominated by the lower vibrational partner, the lower vibrational partner is still ennobled by the association, but the higher vibrational partner has been brought down.

So, it is a question of dominance. It is a question of rightful leadership. It is a question of the appropriateness of what it is to be dominant.

If the higher vibrational decisions of the human dominate over the animal passions of the human, then the entire human including the lower passions are raised, are ennobled. But, if the lower vibrational animal passions are victorious and consume the higher vibration, the lower passions have still been ennobled, but the higher vibration has been brought low.

If one is dominated by the animal passions consistently, over a period of time, then the spirit that goes forward from one incarnation to the next is carrying some heavy baggage in its 'cache' of memory. And, instead of stepping up vibrationally from one incarnation to another, instead of learning more complex lessons, instead of having more control and more choice, the opposite is true. The spirit steps down in vibration and comes to a place where free will choice is more structured and more strictured, for you don't give a two year old a loaded gun. And, if a grad student who would be worthy of the loaded gun, regresses to the point of a two year old, you don't let him say, "I'll take that gun now." The person must mature first to a position where he or she can be trusted with it.

As the animal nature is raised in vibration, it tends to become less resistant to the leadership of the spiritual. It is slow progress instead of swift progress. Yet, one can grow by leaps and bounds even in a single incarnation. That was true before my time, as well as after my time.

Yes, I've had a role to play. I've continued to play the role, and my role has been to support a swift growth of humanity beyond the pace of the growth that humanity experienced before my coming. Yet, let us not forget that the Buddha and other teachers before me played similar roles. There are differences between our roles and lifetimes, yet there are also similarities in that we came to bring that great leap forward that otherwise might have taken thousands more years of slow growth to accomplish.

What is the single factor that stimulates the growth speed up? Light. Light is vibration. So, I came to 'bring the Light' even as there are people today in smaller ways going into dark places to bring the Light.

Passage 8

*And he said: "Man is like a skilful fisherman, casting his
net into the sea and drawing it out replete with small fish.
If the wise fisherman finds amongst them a large fish he
throws the smaller back into the sea, having selected the
largest with ease. He who has ears to hear, let him hear."*

This passage is about recognizing priorities and
getting to the heart of importance. It means in part...don't
sweat the small stuff! When you have all these little fish
and concerns in your net, and there's one big one, take care
of the big one. There are many layers of meaning in this.
The other thing is, when you have a group you are seeking
to influence or exert leadership experience over, go to the
one who is already the leader and persuade him or
overcome him and the rest will take care of itself.

It also has to do with conservation. Allow the little
ones to grow up and there will be plenty of fish in the sea.
Take the one who is ready to be taken instead of feeding on
the juveniles. It is like in the old west, you don't want to
shoot the innocent women and children. If you're going to
have a gunfight, you have it with another gunfighter. Don't
go about defeating little creatures smaller than yourself – or
consuming them – unless it is their role to be consumed.

It means take the greater glory rather than
repetitions of small glory. It also means take the greater
challenge rather than repeating lessons that have already
been successfully learned.

As far as 'who has ears let him hear,' that is a saying
that I have used again and again which means if you are

discerning and you perceive the meaning of it, then listen up and absorb the wisdom. And, it also means that I acknowledge there may be those present who do not have ears to hear it, and so it is not meant for them. It is meant for those who have the discernment, the ears to hear it.

Passage 9

Jesus said, "A sower came forth, filled his hands, and cast.
A few seeds fell upon the road, where birds came down and
devoured them. Others fell among thorns, where they
choked, or were eaten by worms. Still others fell upon
good ground, where they could bring forth good fruit."

This one is often quoted and clearly it has to do with recognizing that not all listeners are equally receptive. Here we go back to the saying often found in the Gospel of Thomas about 'who has ears let him hear.' Who is fertile ground to receive the seed, will receive it. Some people are not fertile ground. You have seen this.

The one most recently known as Mother Teresa is a good example here. Some people look at Mother Teresa and think that of the many seeds she cast, most fell on infertile ground. Yet, she did what she did out of honest, pure joy. And, she did what she did out of karmic motivation which doesn't just mean that she was high and mighty in one lifetime so now she is learning the other side of the lesson. In a previous lifetime, she had been one of the lowest of the low and someone was kind to her. And, she was acknowledging that kindness in the Mother Teresa lifetime while serving as a particular kind of role model.

In any case, that is a pretty obvious interpretation. If I withheld the seeds of my Light, saying, "Well, I can't guarantee that all of these will be used correctly," then I would be choking off life, off creativity, before they even had a chance to begin. But, when I sow my seeds, I know some of them will fall on deaf ears. I know the birds will come and take some of them…well, you see, I don't actually object to that! The birds know to share the Light!

But, I know some of them will fall on stony ground and some of them will fail to germinate and some of them will be eaten by worms…well, I don't really have a problem with the worms either! But, the worms here are symbolic of the seeds that will be consumed by factors or entities for whom they were not intended. And, therefore, they will die without having germinated, grown, and flourished.

Now, let us look at two definitions of fertile ground. Let us suppose this relates to your choices now as human beings. Let us suppose there is a strip of highway…oh, a parking lot is even better. It is 300 feet by 300 feet. In the very middle of this parking lot is one lonely little patch of earth and someone has come along and dug it up and prepared it for planting. I come along with my bag of seeds. I am not going to waste my time sowing the whole parking lot. I am going to go directly to the little patch of fertile earth and plant those seeds with great care, covering and nourishing each one of them.

On the other hand, let us suppose there is a plowed fertile field waiting to be sown, and it is 300 feet by 300 feet. But, in this field there are a few rocky patches here and there. I am not going to plant one seed at a time, carefully over the whole fertile lot, avoiding the few stones. So, how you sow, how you seed your Light depends on your perception of receptivity. Where there are likely to be receptive fertile ground persons, then give generously. Where the receptive persons are very few in a group, don't waste your breath on the group. Seek out those who qualify as fertile ground and put your attention on them.

However, back to our parking lot example. If you cover the asphalt with a thick layer of seeds, they will grow. That's what Mother Teresa was trying to do. She was 'carpet seeding' a whole area. She was taking the long-range view instead of the short-range view. She was saying, "I may not have enough for all of you, but I will provide for as many as I can because I know some of these seeds will pay off and I am making it my cause to convert stony ground to fertile soil."

You have to put everything into its own context. There have to be a few people like Mother Teresa to lead the way in a certain direction. But, I don't expect you to do that. I expect you to focus on priorities because it will advance the overall cause faster. Mother Teresa's approach is not an appropriate path for everyone. It is no more spiritually correct to carpet seed than it is to seed with care.

Passage 10

Jesus said, "I have cast a fire upon the world, and I rekindle it until it burns."

Oh, I love this one. What I said was, "I have brought my fire into the world and cast it to all of you and I keep doing this until you get the message." I have brought the fire of my energy, the Light of my God self. If it seems to go out, I'll run over and light it again until the whole Earth blazes in its glory.

I have observed, on a number of occasions, some people's behavior toward fires. When the fire is on the verge of going out, they come along and shake the heck out of it and stir it up and rekindle the flame until it blazes. It is a wonderful act of abundance consciousness rather than scarcity consciousness. For, scarcity consciousness conserves the wood and only gives enough shaking to get the fire going. This act of abundance reflects the person's love of the experience of fire, and his or her participation in transforming the wood into new forms of energy and life.

Fire is transformation. The energy of my God self is like a fire that burns. I have cast my fire upon the world, and will continually rekindle it to burn away the old to make way for the new.

Passage 11

Jesus said, "This Heaven shall pass away and that above shall pass away. The dead no longer live. The living no longer die. When you ate good things it was you who gave them life. But what are you going to do in the Light? When you were One you were made Two, but when you are two, what are you going to do?"

There are layers of meaning in this passage, so let's break it down. To start with, we have talked about how the earth has layers of vibrational range like the layers of an aura. The early earth to some people may have seemed like heaven, like the Garden of Eden. But this heaven, the heaven they envisioned, the simplistic heaven, would pass away. And, the next one they envisioned, their next higher vision of heaven, would pass away. So, it speaks of the growth of human expectation in that what used to be thought of as heaven, is now too small to contain the human concept of what heaven is. Your ideas today of what heaven is will pass away, and the next set of ideas you have of what heaven is will also pass away. This is one layer of meaning.

The dead are not alive…this means that what has gone before is no longer operational in your life. It means in a way, to stop looking back. And the living will not die…it means the time is coming when death will have new meaning, different meaning. There won't be the old kind of death. This was very true at the time I gave this particular information because among other things, up until that time, there was no universal – that is, applied to everyone – reincarnation. Many of those who lived and died were not reborn as personalities.

It is like the difference between an animal spirit and a human spirit. Some spirits that were unremarkable in their achievements and their vibrational ranges, simply went back into the collective consciousness without retaining individual consciousness perpetuated one lifetime after another. So, 'the dead are not alive' means some of those who have gone before no longer exist now, for their time has come and gone. Yet, those who are living now will not die in that they will reincarnate, they will carry forward into new understanding those aspects of their present day personalities that they have created by experience and learning.

The dead are not alive…what has gone before is finished. But, the living will not die…it is a new beginning. When I came and accomplished my mission, old karma was cleared. That is the sacrificial aspect of what I did. Up until that time, the old law…remember, I said I came not to abolish the law but to fulfill it? I fulfilled the old law by having enough Light to clear not only what might have been called my karma (if I had any), but everyone's. It gave everyone an opportunity for new beginning as a default choice, but it did not take away the individual's right to choose. Some people chose to carry through with their old karma and others let it go, choosing instead a fresh start.

Karma is a way of determining the degree to which the light of Godhood has lodged firmly in the human creature. Even if it is but a tiny spark, if it has lodged securely in the human creature, then that human goes forward to develop the Light, that tiny spark, that it may grow and brighten.

But, the dead who are not alive are those in whom the spark really didn't lodge firmly and there was not much there to carry forward. For, God and God Light and consciousness are very tied together; they are One. How could you bring forward into a new life a lack of consciousness? A lack of consciousness of self. A lack of consciousness of others. A lack of consciousness of self as a vessel of God's own Light. So, those who may have experienced human life as aware but not self aware, there was no need to bring them forward to the next step.

The next part of the passage says that during the days when you ate what was dead, you enlivened it. You gave it purpose and meaning it otherwise might not have had. For, if the meat of the deer is not eaten, it lies there and rots. But, when it sustains a human, because the human is the dominant species upon the planet, then it is fulfilling a role it was brought here and created to play. So, you have enlivened what otherwise would simply be dead meat.

There is a consciousness of the animal that is eaten that is species group consciousness, and it does raise the vibration of the species group consciousness to know it is successfully playing an important role. Interaction will have an effect, just as interaction with companion animals that are not eaten also has an effect on the species. The consciousness of the species is enlivened by its association with humanity, even if the nature of association with humanity has to do with eating and being eaten.

When you are in the Light, what will you do? I'm looking for a way to explain it…ah! They've left out a part of that verse, that's my problem. When you are enlightened, what will you do? Will you be the eaten or eater? Will your vibration be so high that even the foods you eat will be enlivened by your use of them, or will your vibration be so low that the only way you can rise is to be consumed by a higher being? And, the word 'eat' here…consumed would perhaps be a better translation, for there are those who are consumed by God, for instance.

So, will you be the consumer or the consumed?

On the day when you were One, you became two. But, when you become two, what will you do? On the day when you were One, when there was but one consciousness, you become two, your consciousness separated. This speaks of the...well, some religious people would call it the fall of man, or the fall of angels into flesh who then became man, but it speaks of in what the Edgar Cayce readings are called the First Cause and Second Cause. When you were One that is the First Cause. When you became two, that is the Second Cause which is Godhood choosing to experience itself. And, it is also the moment of creation. You might say Second Cause is/was the big bang.

Passage 12

*The disciples said to Jesus, "We know that you will go
away from us; who will become great over us?" Jesus
said, "To whatever place you have come, you will go to
James the righteous; Heaven and earth came into being for
him."*

       What I was saying basically was that my Light
burns brightly in James. Wherever you are, if you are
troubled and if you cannot hear me speak in your own heart
directly, then go to James.
       I spoke relatively easily through James. He had
been with me and speaking as I was speaking then, he
understood me. His concept of justice was like my own
and they could trust him to give a just answer, a wise
answer to their questions. When I said wherever you are go
to him, it also meant remember him, as well as me, and
think what he would have said. He was quite a diplomat,
and sometimes he had a way of expressing my thoughts and
words as he repeated them that amplified or explained them
to the people. When I wasn't reaching people, they would
say to James, "What did he say? What did he mean by
that? Can you tell us what we're supposed to make of
this?" For all my humanity, sometimes my Godhood led
me to take some shortcuts, and I might not remember in my
human sense what I had said or not said. James was very
good in the ability to rephrase, and he had an excellent
memory.
       What they've left out of this verse is that I said, "If
you must have a leader, go to James the Just." They took

out the qualifying phrase 'if you must have a leader.' I knew that true leadership was within each of them, and yet, I also understood they may not have been confident enough yet to hear that true answer. They wanted to feel they were not going to be alone after I left, so I said you could always talk things over with James. He'll understand. And, when I said for him heaven and earth were made, I was saying that my Light shines brightly in him. He is a part of the Christ Light, the Christ consciousness, and for this, heaven and earth were made.

Earth was made for the great experiment. The great experiment was to see whether the God consciousness could successfully be lodged in the animal form. And why was heaven made? Well, think about what they meant by heaven in that day and time. They meant that envelope of spiritual energy and spiritual interaction that was the highest earth could envision or reach at the time.

For people today, if you can remember the phrase that was left out, 'if you must have a leader,' then go to someone who is wise and just in whom the Light shines brightly, who has a close association with the All, who has the Christ consciousness. For, the term Christ consciousness means more than the Christ. It is the state of being enlightened as Christ was enlightened and as I became enlightened. And, for this Christ consciousness, heaven and earth were made.

Passage 13

Jesus said to his disciples, "Make a comparison and tell who I am like." Simon Peter said to him, "You are like a righteous angel." Matthew said to him, "You are like a wise man." Thomas said to him, "Master, my mouth will not be able to say what you are like." Jesus said, "I am not your master because you drank; you are drunk from the bubbling spring which I measured." And he took him; he went aside. He spoke to him three words. When Thomas returned to his companions, they asked him, "What did Jesus say to you?" Thomas said to them, "If I tell you one of the words which he said to me, you will pick up stones; you will throw them at me. And fire will come from the stones and consume you."

I said to them, "What do you think of me? How do I seem to you? Compare me to something and tell me what your vision of me is." So, Simon Peter looked upon me and said, "I know you are a true and just messenger of God for when you speak I hear the words of God and I see their Godly source. Like an angel, you are a true messenger. You are the true vessel bearing the message of the Light." And, of course, that is true.

Matthew looked at me and knew that sometimes when people asked me questions, I would stop and think, "How can I best answer this question in a way the questioner can receive the answer." A philosopher, one who loves wisdom, will take the time and trouble to do what he can to make it accessible to the others, to someone who has asked a question. Someone who loves wisdom will not deliberately make his answer obscure and inaccessible. That is what Matthew was saying he saw in me. He saw not only my ability, but also my desire and intent as a lover of wisdom, to render Godly wisdom accessible to the listener.

Thomas was saying to me, "I have no words. There is nothing I can use to compare you to. I have no words to say what I see in you, for these are wonders beyond my ability to clothe the idea in words." And, he called me 'rabbi' which of course means teacher, because that was the role I played.

I went on to say to Thomas, "I am the vessel, not the source. It is not from my own wisdom as a human being that I teach you. It is that the bubbling spring, the waters of life, the living water of God Light has filled you and you have drunk from it. You have taken it in. I have tended this spring. I have helped make it accessible to you. You didn't have to dig for it. I brought it to the surface where you could bend and drink from it. You didn't have to pull the leaves and twigs out of it, or the small insects. I used the net and cleared it for you. (Which metaphorically speaking, means that you didn't have to figure out what is truth and what is falsehood. I cleaned it up for you so there is only clarity; there is only truth.) I have tended this spring, this great outpouring of the water of life, which of course is life, is energy. And, you are intoxicated with it."

What does intoxication mean? It means to be in an altered state of consciousness. And because he had drunk deeply, he had taken the water of life, the Light, the energy into himself, he was in an altered state of consciousness in which he could see and hear and feel things for which he had no words.

So, I said to Thomas, "Come. Let's have a private talk." And, I took him and embraced him and raised the vibration of his human shell in such a way as to prevent it from being burned up, consumed by the fire of knowledge of the Light. And I showed him more and I said, "Look. This is who I am. I am God." And, I said, "Look. This is who you are. You are God." And, I said, "Look upon the others. Even though they do not know it yet, they are Gods. You will come, in time, to know the truth of this." But, even without knowing the truth of it, as he would come in time to do, he could feel it. And, so, when he went back to the others, he was coming down from a pretty tall high.

They said, "Tell us, tell us! What did he say to you?" And, Thomas said, "If I told you one tiny bit of what he said to me, you would be angry." He realized they would think it was blasphemy. They would doubt I said it to him. They would think he was making it up. So, he was looking at the credibility issue, and in those days, if you had too big a credibility issue, they would pick up rocks and throw them at you as a sign of disapproval. Fortunately, this particular way of expressing disapproval has fallen out of fashion…at least in most modern societies!

Thomas was saying to them, "If I told you even a small part of this, you wouldn't believe me and you would reject me, because what I have heard from our brother Jesus is so far away from what you now believe you could not accept it. You would stone me. And, if you stoned me, then the stones themselves would rise up against you. For, the stones themselves, the very fabric of the earth, know the Light."

People still struggle with the 'I am God' issue. Even those we might call the spiritually enlightened people. If you sit there and look them straight in the eye and say, "I am God," they will reject it. They will say it is ego. Do you know why? Because they think God is an egotistical being. So, when you say 'God,' they say, "Oh, so you think you are great and powerful, stronger, and more wonderful and wiser than anybody else?" They believe God is egotistical. They believe God gets off on being better than everybody else. It is the limited human idea of who and what God is. So, yes, they are rejecting your claim to Godhood, but they are also in their own strange way validating your claim to Godhood. They think, when you say, "I am God," that you are behaving in an egotistical way just like God does. It is a bit of an oxymoron.

Yet, this rejection has an even deeper effect, for when they reject the God light in others, they are also rejecting it within themselves.

Passage 14

Jesus said to them, "If you fast, you will bring sin upon yourselves and, if you pray, you will condemn yourselves, and, if you give alms, you will do evil to your spirits. And if you enter any land and wander through the regions, if they receive you, whatever they set before you, eat it. Heal the sick among them. For that which goes in your mouth will not defile you, but that which comes out of your mouth is what will defile you."

The meaning is: if you fast thinking that is what is required of you, you will bring sin unto yourself, because fasting is not what it is all about. If you give to charity and think that by having done so you have fulfilled your spiritual obligation, you will have done yourself a spiritual injury because giving to charity, although it is a good thing, is not what it's all about. One should give to charity and one should fast for one's own personal reasons - if at all - and not as a way of becoming eligible for a free pass straight to heaven.

If you pray, you will be condemned. If you beg God to do everything for you, God will say, "Why aren't you doing it for yourself?" This is the difference between prayer and being in tune with God. Praying presupposes that God is great and the human is small and that God can grant anything and the human can do nothing unless God grants it. That is a very low vibrational, old-fashioned way of looking at the relationship between God and humanity.

Many times in the Bible, and in virtually all religious literature, God is characterized as a loving father.

A loving father provides for his children that which they are as yet unable to provide for themselves. This includes such things as the basic necessities of food, shelter, cleanliness, etc. There comes a time when the infant becomes more aware and self-aware, and may see something like a bottle of milk and think, "I want that." The infant will 'pray' for it by making his or her wants and needs known and the mother or father responds by providing the desired item. It is an 'answer to prayer.' Sometimes a prayer is the word 'no' as in: please make it stop. "No, no, no. Something is hurting me. Please make it stop." It is still a request from one who cannot do it for himself, to have the parent do it for him.

Now, as the child grows, what does the parent say when the child demands, "I want my bear"? The parent says, "Go get it yourself." The wise parent encourages independence in the child. So, if you stand there and pray and say, "God grant me this. Oh, I pray for that. I pray, I pray, I pray..." and you do nothing to help make your prayer come true, then you will be condemned for having misunderstood the nature of your relationship to the mother/father God. For God is not a control freak. God does not want the responsibility of telling every human what to do, all the time - much less of doing everything for the human, all the time.

God helps those who help themselves. God encourages those who help themselves. God favors and smiles upon those who help themselves. Haven't you noticed that luck seems to favor those who work for it? There is another human saying: "Luck is little more than the residue of hard work." So, again, if you pray, if you only come to beg and don't do anything but beg, you will be condemned. If you only say, "Oh, Lord, won't you buy me a Mercedes Benz," you will be condemned for the shallow, unempowered, and utterly selfish prayer you have

48

uttered.

When you go to another country where, perhaps, the people's customs are not like your own, and their dietary customs are not like your own, don't be holier-than-thou or squeamish. Don't make a fool of yourself in front of these strangers by asking for delicacies they cannot provide, or by ostentatiously fasting and making a big deal of how holy you are in your eating habits. Eat what they put before you. Allow yourself to be one of them. For, in doing so, you will become accepted. Talk to them. Find out what their needs are. Go among them teaching and healing and help to meet their needs. You can't do that as a holier-than-thou, egotistical outsider. To do it, you must become one of them. It isn't what you eat that defiles you. It's what you *do* and *say* that can defile you.

You can't change things from the outside. You change things from the inside. Why would I have come into flesh if things didn't need to be changed from the inside? I didn't want to just come along tapping people on the head with a magic wand. It's not enough. I wanted people to see it for themselves and to feel it for themselves. Like a good father, a good mother, I wanted my children to truly learn and grow, to become wise, to become responsible, to mature. And, that comes from the inside out.

Passage 15

*Jesus said, "When you see him who was not born of
woman, throw yourself down on your face (and) adore him;
that one is your father."*

When you see a thought form manifestation such as
Michael or Melchizedek, you see someone who is clearly
more than human, who does not have the characteristics of
humanity, the limitations of humanity, but someone who
simply is. I am what I am.

Remember the distinction we make between angels
and humans...the angels have never been incarnate, yet
they have walked the earth many times. And, there is
something about them, in that they are vessels of Light in a
way the flesh cannot contain. So, people feel that
difference and when they see an angel, usually they know it
is not an ordinary mortal. When you see someone who is an
embodiment of Light, of the energy, fall down and worship
for this is truly your Father. This is truly the source of your
Light. This is truly God, for God is Light. God is energy.

When you see that power, even if it comes in the
illusion of a human form, know it for what it is and respond
to it. Give it the highest recognition that you are capable of
giving. Perhaps an innocent, pure and high vibrational
child might see such a vision from a little distance and
come running and leap, throwing himself or herself into it.
It is the highest response the child is capable of giving.
Wanting to be a part of the Light.

A great many people, even now, are not ready to be
a part of it to the degree of jumping right in. Do you know

why not? They fear they might not come back out. They are afraid to lose the 'incarnate' life, which is the only life they truly know. So, I say to these people to accept the manifestation of Light in whatever form it might take, in a way that it can become a part of their incarnate experience. Be open to an experience of Light at a higher level and learn to recognize the Light when it is before you.

Passage 16

Jesus said, "Men might think I have come to throw peace on the world, and they do not know that I have come to throw dissolution on the earth; fire, sword, war. For there shall be five in a house: three shall be against two and two against three, the father against the son and the son against the father, and they shall stand as solitaries."

Some people think I have come to impose peace upon the world. The operative word here is 'impose.' It is just like I said in a previous passage; it is not enough to satisfy me that I should come and just tap people on the head and make them do what I think is a good idea. That was never the purpose. It is contrary to free will, which is vested in humanity.

So, I came to inspire people to learn and grow. How do people learn and grow? Through conflict. Through experience. Through trying on different ideas for size. Through disagreement people learn to reach an agreement. You know how light brightens the dark corners and that which was hidden, is no longer hidden, and must be dealt with. You know how it is that Light energy makes people antsy and uncomfortable. You know how it is that Light brings up old issues and conflicts within an individual – much less if you have a group of people to deal with!

The Light itself is a stimulus. Then come the fires, and people get very wrought up about their illusionary belief systems. People get fired up about what they want. One of the things that has started wars the most is wanting what someone else has. Or, your perception that someone else is trying to take what is yours. Even today in the land of Israel, the violence, the wars, the struggle and conflict are about territorial perception. The Jews want what they believe to be theirs. The Palestinians want what they believe to be theirs. And each of them has the perception that says the other is trying to take it from him.

There is no way to truly have what is yours without giving it up and recognizing that it belongs to everyone. Issues of ownership among those who have something, who own things, are giving way to issues of stewardship – what do you do with it? The idea of passing from ownership – it's mine, I'll do what I want with it, I'll destroy it if I wish – is passing to ownership that says, "I need to own this so I can take care of it and prevent someone else from harming it." It's a concept of moving from ownership for exploitation to ownership for stewardship. That's a big step in the right direction.

Conflict comes from perceptions of limitation. Scarcity consciousness. It comes from the idea that someone can take it away from you. And, of course, as long as you are enrolled in that way of thinking, someone *can* take it away from you. As long as you are invested and enrolled in the maya, the illusion of concrete possessions as the only objects of value, then someone can take them away from you.

Look at Viktor Frankl, holocaust survivor, who said there's only one thing no one can take away from me. They can take my possessions. They can take my money. They can take my dignity. They can take my comfort. They can take my life. The only thing I have that they can't take is my attitude, my choice to choose how I feel. There are a lot of people out there who haven't gotten that message yet.

The part of this passage that talks about conflict

within a house, a family, speaks of how it is human nature, the nature of the growing, learning, but not-yet-there humans, to disagree among themselves. If you have five people, how are you going to get them all to agree? They'll be three on one side and two on the other. Father and son will disagree – it's called the generation gap. The father doesn't like being taken out of his comfort zone and the son says, "Let's go out and stir up some excitement!"

And, they shall stand alone. This means basically, I'm not coming in to do it for them. They must learn to stand on their own two feet. And they shall stand on their own two feet. They shall learn to stand alone.

If I imposed peace upon the world, then I would be the caretaker, not the teacher. So, I came instead to stimulate growth. And, stimulating growth means there will be conflict. It is the fire of life to experience – to burn with ideas. Not to burn as in pain, but to burn with the drive and passion to experience life. And certainly I had every intention of bringing that kind of fire into the world. The fire of creation. The fire that burns away impurities. The fire of transformation.

Passage 17

Jesus said, "I will give you what no eye has seen and what no ear has heard and no hand has touched and what has not come into the heart of man."

I like this one, if I do say so myself. I said to them, "What I have to give you is not something you can see or hear or touch. You can't grab hold of it. It is an idea. It is intangible. I come in revelation and transformation to give you the energy – to give you the intangible in a way that it is made accessible to you." The intangible, the energy, was all around them before I came, but they could not receive it from the air.

Their eyes could not perceive it, to see it and take it in. Their ears couldn't perceive it, to hear it and take it in. Their hands could not perceive it, to touch it, to hold it and take it in. They were not prepared to receive direct energy. They had to receive it from someone in a human body. They would receive from one who was one of them. And, I was one of them. In becoming one of them, they opened themselves to become one with me. And so, they stood before God able to receive what, up until that time, no truly human heart had known.

That by the way, is one of the differences between my coming as a teacher, and a shower of the way, and the other great teachers such as the Buddha, Mohammed, and Lao Tsu. The others were, for the most part, teachers of wisdom and understanding and did not, in the same way, carry the energy and share it at the heart level. I radiated the heart principle, the principle of love. This is, of course, not to say that I was not a part of these great teachers and all the rest. It was just a different approach for a certain time period in earth's history. The closest thing to my coming was a long time before, in Krishna and Shiva for they also brought the fire, the passion. They brought the energy to more than just the heart chakras, and they are seen in Hindu mythology as savior figures, as those who brought the Light and the fire.

For me, I carried an energy, a Light, that the human heart of those who chose to be open was capable of receiving directly. Think of the people I healed. It was by their acceptance of my Light that it happened.

If you will stop and think about it, the word 'compassion' relates to this. Com-passion - to feel with. It is the difference between the spirit of the law and the letter of the law. It means receive the Light, don't just think about it and become perfect in that way. But, let it in and be transformed. It is transformation. That is the meaning of grace, as opposed to salvation by works.

Passage 18

The disciples said to Jesus, "Tell us in which way our end will occur." Jesus said, "Have you found the beginning that you search for the end? In the place where the beginning is, there the end will be. Blessed is he who will stand at the beginning, and he will know the end and he will not taste death."

This is another one with layered meaning. When they said, "Tell us where it will all end," I said, "At the beginning. It is alpha and omega. It will end as it began, as a grand mystery of Oneness. All is One. All is God."

And then I said, "Do you really think you have found the beginning already so you are looking for the end?" I was saying, in effect, you are asking a small question – a small-minded question. You are asking, where are we going to end up? And, I am saying your work has not even yet begun. How can you know where you're going to end up, when you haven't yet put your feet on the path?

History is prologue. All that I am teaching you is not the beginning. You have not begun your work. All that I am teaching you is preparation for the beginning. When you have begun your work, when you have made the decisions about how you will use what I have taught you, then you will see where it must lead. And, as you see where it must lead, you will know you are on a journey toward nirvana, and you will not taste death…for there is only life of one kind or another.

Passage 19

Jesus said, "Blessed is he who was before he was created.
If you become my disciples (and) you hear my words, these
stones shall serve you. For you have five trees in paradise
which do not move in summer or winter and they do not
shed their leaves. Whoever knows them shall not taste
death."

Fortunate is he who came into being before coming into being. Fortunate is she who has experienced consciousness in such a way that it has carried forward into her present lifetime. Fortunate is he who has lived before, who perhaps even has lived in distant realms before he came to this earth, yet who retained the essence of himself. Fortunate is she who, in having a preexisting Light body, now illumines the physical body with that Light which was hers before she was born. Fortunate is he who has something to bring to this incarnation and to this planet.

Follow me and you will move into energies, states of consciousness, states of awareness, states of being that you in your present form of humanity have only dreamt of. The humans to whom I spoke in those times, had not dreamt of transformation as you have. If God had sent them such a dream, they would have thought it was entirely symbolic. They never would have accepted the idea that they could actually be transformed. Follow me and you will experience joyful wonders beyond the ability of unenlightened humanity to receive them, to embrace them, to know them, to feel them, to be them.

We have talked about not tasting the bitterness of

death in an earlier passage. In this particular instance, speaking to the people in that particular time, the five trees of paradise were the five senses. I wanted to say to them, "You don't have to be afraid of death, for there is only life ahead of you. And in that life which is more vibrant, more beautiful, which is greater than the life you have now, there are five trees. There are sight, hearing, taste, smell and touch. And they do not wither or die. If you were blind on the earth, yet you shall see in paradise. If you were deaf upon the earth, yet you shall hear in paradise. If you were insensate upon the earth, you will feel every touch in paradise."

These trees of the five senses are there for you. I was saying, "You will experience in paradise – in the afterlife, what comes after death – you will experience the tangible things that have meaning to you. They are there for you and you shall not taste death."

Think of what these people thought the tasting of death meant. They thought it meant annihilation. They thought it meant, at best, being disembodied. Think of what people consider the tasting of death today is – many of them still fear it is annihilation, and by far the greater part of humanity believes that it is, at the very least, disembodiment in which they will not have sight, hearing, taste, smell and touch.

Being on the other side does not bring you less; it brings you more. Everything you have in this incarnation you will still have access to – and more besides. The next world is not more limited; it is less limited. It is the principle of receiving more and more as you go along instead of less and less. And, of course, that is the whole idea I was trying to get across to these people about paradise. And, I was speaking of reincarnation as well as the ultimate paradise or heaven.

If you become my followers, remember that my

purpose here was to show the way. My message to humanity summed up in a single phrase is, "Follow me." Set yourself upon the path of learning. Accept the Light, as I accept the Light. Become the Light, as I am the Light. That's why I chose to be human. To show that a human can do it.

Follow me. If I did it, so can you.

Passage 20

The disciples said to Jesus, "Tell us, what the Kingdom of Heaven is like?" He said to them, "It is like a mustard seed, smaller than all seeds. But when it falls on plowed ground, it puts forth a large branch and becomes a shelter for the birds of heaven."

They said, "Tell us what heaven is like." And I said, "It is the smallest, like a mustard seed." The mustard seed I was referring to here is just a metaphor for smallness – and how even smallness can contain everything. The potential is there. But, if you expect heaven to be no more than a simple green field with a stream running through it, then that will be your heaven and you will never look beyond it for more.

When the idea of heaven, of paradise, falls upon fertile soil, and that being a metaphor for the idea of heaven is planted in someone who has an imagination, then you have this wonderful, co-creative force that comes into being, and a new vision of paradise is created out of the marriage between human imagination and God Light of self-empowerment. This is co-creatorship.

When I speak of a tree that birds of heaven can roost in, it means that the worlds created by the co-creatorship human idea of what heaven should be like, will populate these new heavens. You know very well humans have directly contributed to creating so many visions of paradise. So many visions of life – simple and complex. Think about Ann McCaffrey's world of Pern. Maybe it isn't some people's idea of heaven, but then again, there are some people who would look at it and say, "Sure looks like heaven to me." A place that is beautiful, but not entirely dull.

You know, a lot of modern humans think of paradise as a pretty dull place. They might not stop to define it that way, but their vision of it is like that mustard seed – a tiny vision of a tiny imagination. But when you plant the same seed of knowledge of experience on more fertile ground – that is, in someone with a more fertile imagination – then the heavens, the cosmos, the universe are exponentially enriched by what this animal god, this god-animal hybrid being of humanity has brought forth.

Passage 21

Mary said to Jesus, "Whom are your disciples like?" He said, "They are like little children; they settle themselves in a field that is not theirs. When the owners of the field come they (the owners) say, 'Give us our field.' They undress before them and release it (the field) to them and give back their field to them. Because of this I say, if the owner of the house knows that the thief is coming, he will watch before he comes and will not let him break into his house of his kingdom and carry away his goods. But you watch especially for the world; gird your loins with great power lest the robbers find a way to come upon you, because the thing you expect, they will find. Let there be a man of understanding among you. When the fruit ripened, he came quickly, his sickle in his hand (and) he reaped it. He who has ears, let him hear."

Mary said to me, "What are your followers like?" In other words she said, who are these people who come and follow after you and listen to what you have to say? What do they mean to you, to us? And I said they are like little children in a field – the field being analogous to earth – that does not belong to them. And one of these days they are going to realize it is God's earth, not theirs. And when God comes along and says, "Give me back the earth," they will realize that they can no longer stay in their immaturity, but must move forward to the next step or go back and do the last step over again. In either case, they will realize they don't actually own the field; they can't take it with them. They are moving on.

So they will take off their garments – in other words, they will shed their illusions – and they will leave their property behind and in their nakedness will return the earth to God, the rightful owner. It is a dust to dust, ashes to ashes kind of a statement. Yet, what they take with them is the naked self, the 'who they are' self and all they have experienced, and they then move into another vibration range, into another state of consciousness.

The part about the house and the robber – well, that is the theme of preparedness. If you know what is coming, be prepared. And what I was talking about here was the loss of consciousness that might follow my crossing and my followers passing out of my spirit influence. Mary and I were actually talking about what comes after, and I was saying we know there will be challenges for them. We know someone will come and try to rob them of their Light. We know someone will come to try and usurp or destroy the 'house' we have built.

You can relate to this even in modern times. When you are in a special space, be it during meditation, enjoying a quiet beach on vacation, or sharing deep moments with a loved one, the challenge is maintaining that special energy when you return to mundane tasks in your daily life. I knew my disciples would be challenged to hold their Light energy after my crossing – once they no longer literally 'walked beside God' and shared my Light.

So, I prepared them as best I could. I prepared my followers to be able to defend themselves against those who would put out their Light, who would rob them of their treasures – and by this, I mean the treasures of understanding. The treasures of knowledge. The treasures of experience that they had built up. I said to them, "Be prepared. You need to understand that it is better to be prepared, to be foresighted. Like a man whose house is about to be robbed, if you know the house is about to be robbed, you can take measures to deal with it ahead of time."

Of course, as you well know, the robbers did come and they did usurp the house that I had built. They did take it and use it for their own interests. And in that sense, 'robber' simply means someone who took the ideas and turned them to his or her own benefit rather than making an honest effort to honor the original intention. But everyone gets misquoted. Everybody's good teachings get trampled on by time, translation, misuse and by personal agenda. It was inevitable that it would happen to my words.

The last part of the passage that talks about the crop ripening means that at the peak of youthful maturity, when the time is right, that is the moment to harvest what you have and move on. I reached that point and was harvested. Each of my followers, those who devoted themselves to teaching what I had taught and carried the messages into the world, each of them came to a time of maturity and was harvested.

To be left to rot in the fields after you are overripe is no honor. Those who were martyred – think about Peter who was on his way out of Rome until I spoke through the boy. Until I channeled and said, "Where are you going?" And he said, in effect, "I'm getting the hell out of Dodge!" And, I said, "So, you're leaving. Do I need to come back to Rome and be crucified? Someone has to finish the job here. If you aren't going to do it, who will it be? I can't do all of it for you, all the time." And, he understood, and went back and gave himself to be crucified. He gave himself to be harvested because it was time. It was an act of great courage and self-awareness.

The conjunction of events – world events and personal events – came together. That is when the field of grain is ready. If Peter had been cut down sooner, that wouldn't have been harvesting. But, if he had not gone back to Rome to be crucified, but had gone on into some other part of the world and hadn't made the statement of faith that he did, that would have been the equivalent of falling into decay and rotting in the field. For, there is but one moment of peak timing for the harvest.

So, I was saying the time will come for each of us to be harvested. The time will come when each of us must give way to the next wave, the next crop, to make room for the next group of seedlings to grow and mature toward their own harvest. In a farming community, people understand one crop is harvested and then the chaff, the leftover material is plowed under and the field is sowed with seed again. It is the cycle of life.

The cycle of life repeating itself is the unendingness of life. Unending life does not mean crystallization of the moment. It means unending growth and there comes a point where growth must go into the next cycle. So basically, if you are not growing, it's time to be harvested.

Think about the nursing homes. Can you not see the people lying in a vegetative state in those beds are rotting in the fields? Overripe? Or think of a child who says, "I have fulfilled the purpose I came to fulfill. It is time to move on." Perhaps the child served as a stimulus so others could experience grief and learn to overcome it. The child says, "I'm ready to be harvested."

Think of some poor sucker who has really messed up his life. This person looks around and then says to the higher self, "Well, you know what? It's not going to get any better! If we let this incarnation go on, it could even get worse! So, let's just bite the bullet, cut our losses, and declare the harvest." It doesn't matter the age.

Never-ending life has within it cycles of harvest, and new beginnings. The difference is that the 'harvest' does not presuppose the death of a physical body, either because there is no physical body to die or because the physical body is transformed and carried forward. Or, if you want to think of it this way, the physical body might be like a costume of one who has played many roles and that is hung in the wardrobe to be put on or taken off again if one may wish.

The harvest is the recognition of what has come to pass, the implementation, the new seeding, the cyclical growth pattern that is a part of never ending life. Learn not to fear the time of harvest. Instead see it as the next step into a more expanded consciousness and experience of life.

Passage 22

Jesus saw children being suckled. He said to his disciples, "These children who are being suckled are like those who enter the Kingdom." They said to him, "We are children, shall we enter the Kingdom?" Jesus said to them, "When you make the two one, and when you make the inner as the outer and the outer as the inner and the upper as the lower, so that you will make the male and female into a single one, so that the male will not be male and the female (not) be female, when you make eyes in the place of an eye, and hand in place of a hand, and a foot in the place of a foot, (and) an image in the place of an image, then you shall enter [the Kingdom]."

When they saw the nursing babies I said to them, "These little babes are like those in the kingdom of heaven. Their needs are met direct from source." And the source, in this instance, was the mother whose milk feeds them, and as they nurse they also receive the auric energy of the mother and the love the mother has to offer. Those babies who were being nursed all had loving mothers. In those days, if the mother had not loved the child, the child would have been abandoned and would have died, or would have simply been killed and discarded. You may be sure that those babies we saw nursing were all wanted and loved.

So, I was saying those babies are the way you will be in the kingdom. Completely loved, your every need supplied and the Light energy surrounding you, filling you completely. You will be at peace as these children are at peace. You will be completely safe, as these children feel completely safe. You will be content, for your needs are being satisfied, as these babies are content. Your being in the kingdom is like the state of these completely satisfied babies who are safe, loved and cared for in every way.

They also said, "Are we going to be children when we enter the kingdom?" They were thinking of the image of the child, and I was trying to tell them that it's not really how it works. It's not that you will be born into the kingdom as a child is born.

Instead, when the inner becomes as the outer and the outer becomes as the inner, when the inner Light fills you completely and your outer self is vibrationally adjusted to the inner Light within, when there are no gender perceptions or stations between you, when there is no duality, there is only Oneness, then you will know that is the kingdom. When you are able to create what you want on demand – if the foot were gone you could just put another one in its place – when your Godly Light has manifested, then you will know the kingdom.

The part about male and female becoming a single one was a reference to gender distinctions. Gender distinctions in the days in which I spoke these words, were extremely powerful and they were enforced by the teachings of the religions of the day. So, I was saying in part, you're going to have to overcome your stereotypical attitudes if you want to experience the kingdom.

The passage is about duality and it's passing away. Once you have achieved Oneness in yourself, then you do experience the kingdom of heaven. No matter where you are it is there with you because, you have found it and released it within yourself. Heaven is not a place; it is a state of being.

Passage 23

Jesus said, "I shall choose you, one from a thousand, and two from ten thousand, and they shall stand; they are a single one."

I shall choose you, one from a thousand and two from ten thousand and they shall stand as a single one. When I have chosen you and you are in my heart and in my Light, we become One. Yet, only one in a thousand or two in ten thousand are ready to be chosen. It goes back to another biblical phrase, "Many are called and few are chosen." Those who are chosen will have passed through certain initiations and…well, you might say tests, before the choice is made.

Those who are called the apostles, together with certain others of my dear companions, were chosen before any of us were born into incarnation. We were a team in the making, and being born into incarnation was a final launching of the project that we had committed ourselves to as a team. Each person had his and her own role to play. And, each had the potential for playing multiple roles, different roles in case the primary player of any given role stepped out.

So, very few were chosen, and when I spoke those words, I was speaking not of the apostles or my close companions who already were a part of my heart. I was speaking of the next wave that would follow. And, I was saying through Thomas and James and John, and through the other apostles, that I would choose those who would carry forth our work, our project into the next level. And there would be but a handful. Anything more would have been unmanageable with the resources that we had available at that time on the human level.

Those who are called come near to listen, to consider and decide, by their own free will, whether they want to be a part of what I am doing. Do you think I would choose someone who didn't want to come? Do you think I would choose someone who wanted to be chosen but for all the wrong reasons? So, it will only be one in a thousand or two in ten thousand or one in a million, or however you want to put it. It will only be a few whom I choose to bond with me in a deeper and more complete way.

Passage 24

His disciples said, "Show us the place where you are, for it is necessary for us to seek it." He said to them, "He who has ears to hear let him hear. There is light within a man of light and he (or, it) lights the whole world. When he (or, it) does not shine, there is darkness."

You know, I found myself again and again explaining to them that 'where I am' is a metaphor for who I am. It is not a geographical location. When I said to them, "You know, one of these days you're going to be where I am," it was so hard for them – even my close companions – to understand the term 'where' as a metaphor rather than as a fixed point on a map.

I said to them, "Where I go, you will follow." And, so they were saying, "Where is it you're going? Where are you? Tell us so we can come with you." When I said to them that I'm going away, then they said, "Well, tell us where you are going to be so we can come and find you!" If I had said I'm going to die, it would not have been true, for I did not die except for the three days. They would have misunderstood that in an entirely different way. When I said that I'll be going away, I was trying to give the understanding to them that though I am gone away, I am always with you and will always be with you for I am the Light and the Light shines everywhere day and night. In the light places and in the dark places, there is the life force, the energy. And, that is 'where' I am.

It is where the I AM presence has always been and will always forever be, without end. For, it is in every tiny fragment or bit of energy. It is Light. Sadly, so many people still don't understand this message.

Passage 25

Jesus said, "Love your brother as your soul; keep him as the apple of your eye."

Love your brother like your soul. Recognize that your brother is a part of your own soul. It has to do with breaking down barriers and recognizing the value of someone else. If you love your soul, love your brother. You can't really become more soulful, more spiritual unless you learn to appreciate the value and roles of others. The term appreciate here is more appropriate than the word love since I don't mean in this passage to have Eros love, to physically desire another. But, to cherish, care for, and appreciate your brother as you cherish, care for, and appreciate your own soul. For, the two are closely tied together, your appreciation of your brother and your desire for spiritual growth.

I was speaking against separation and speaking for coming together instead of going farther apart. And, to guard this acceptance of others as the pupil of your eye as it is a part of your Light and your view of eternity. The eye is how you see things. Protect this as a viewpoint of how you see eternal life.

74

Passage 26

Jesus said, "The chip that is in your brother's eye you see, but the log in your own eye you do not see. When you take the log out of your eye, then you will see to remove the chip from your brother's eye."

Clearly it is easier to see someone else's faults than your own. It is easy to see the faults in someone else's religion, for instance, than it is to see the even greater and more glaring faults in one's own. But, if you come to the point of being enlightened, if you remove the great blockage from your own viewpoint, then you will be in a much better position to assist someone else in removing the smaller blockage from his or her vision.

This is along the same line as, "Healer, heal thyself." And, it is along the same line as saying, to be a good counselor, you must have done the work on yourself. Every psychiatrist and psychologist who is trained by the traditional system, has been through psychoanalysis. It is just part of the process.

Many great teachers of figure skating were figure skaters at one point, and they know not only how it looks to be a skater, but they know something about how it feels to be a skater. There is also the New Age phrase, "You teach what you most need to learn." We have talked about how people prepare themselves to be good counselors, and it is not just by becoming wiser by dealing with their own problems, but there is also the factor of being able to identify with the client or the student.

Many of those people who specialize now in drug or alcohol counseling are recovering alcoholics or drug addicts. Many of those now who counsel incestuous abuse victims, were themselves incestuously sexually abused. This gives them not only insight – compassion – in how it feels, but it gives them the proof that they have the compassion, for they can say, "I've been there."

Again and again, you have heard me say that you have to be able to say 'been there, done that' for some people to take you seriously as an advisor, as a wisdom figure. So, it is more than just a safeguard to keep your own ego from getting in the way, or your own lack of compassion. It is a created credibility that helps people find it easier to listen to you.

The basic meaning of the statement is quite simple. It means…well, there are psychologists who say that all memory is subjective. Remember, there are several kinds of memory. The least subjective is eidetic, but most people don't have eidetic memories, photographic memories. Most people have memories that are far more likely to be subjective. So, when the contamination of your own unclear thinking is brought to bear on someone else's problem, you can't help that person, really. You need to deal with the contamination in your own thinking first. Then, you will be in a much better position to help, even if his or her problem is a lesser one that you, yourself, have overcome.

A lot of people who have specks in their eyes are smart enough to see the beams in other people's vision. There are counselors who project their own stuff, their own interpretation on the counselee, whereas, the counselee may have gotten rid of the beams already, and may just be looking for a clear helper to finish up that last little speck.

Mainly, it means that when your vision is contaminated, your capacity to assist others in helping to clear their vision, is diminished. It also means to examine yourself before you start condemning other people.

Passage 27

"If you do not fast (in respect to) the world, you will not find the Kingdom; if you do not keep the Sabbath a Sabbath, you shall not see the Father."

The key phrase here is to 'respect the world.' If you do not fast, that is if you do not show respect before the world to those persons or institutions that are worthy of respect, then one questions whether your choices are fully appropriate. To rebel outwardly and refuse to show respect is not the same thing as to say, "I will show my respect privately in another way."

For instance, there is a church on the hillside across the street. If this channel goes there during a service, she will do what is expected during the service as a mark of respect to the institution. If this channel visited in a household where fasting for a certain period of time was the rule, she would not, in front of them, sit down to a fine meal and lick her lips as she ate it, for that would be disrespectful to the household. She would fast with them even if privately she had a suitcase full of chocolate!

I chose to be born into a Jewish homeland. I chose to be born into a Jewish family. So, in my Jewish homeland, I observed the laws. The Jews, as everybody knows from the Bible were 'God's chosen people,' and had a communication with Yahweh about numerous things. But, besides that, the Jewish dietary laws for example, were given for good reason. The pork and the other scavengers were contaminated and were 'unclean' – not sacramentally but hygienically. Yet, when I traveled abroad, to India and elsewhere, I didn't make a big deal about keeping the Jewish laws because the audience and the customs weren't the same.

Remember, the kingdom of heaven is within. And, there is a certain measure in which mastery over the self, or self-discipline, is a part of establishing the kingdom within. If you do not fast when it's what you are 'supposed to do,' then it's like cheating. It is dishonorable. It is a lack of self-discipline. A lack of self-respect. And, if you do not keep the customs of the family, tribe, and community into which you have been born, again, it is a lack of self-discipline, a lack of self-respect and a lack of respect for others in your community. Self-discipline, respect for others in your community and self-respect are part of the wisdom training, if you will, and without becoming wise, you will not find the kingdom within you.

People choose to be born into certain situations, sometimes for the discipline, to learn from that particular dynamic. So, the term respect is really a matter of respecting your own choices for experience. One may choose to become a nun or a priest or a monk. There are communities of holy orders in all faiths – Buddhist, Christian, and many others – for whose members being a part of that order requires enormous self-discipline, such as the silent orders where you do not speak. Think how much self-discipline that would require!

So, for someone who needs to be personally convinced that he or she does have self-discipline, joining a silent order and keeping the silence would prove self-discipline to that person. You notice I said, 'prove to that person.' It's really proving it to themselves rather than proving it to me or God or any figure of faith. The kingdom is within, and therefore you must take the steps to the kingdom within yourself.

Follow the customs to the extent that is appropriate to show respect. And as far as keeping the Sabbath, the day of rest might be better called a day of contemplation or introspection. It is a time to withdraw from the world and find peace within one's self. Of course, if you find peace within yourself, then you are at peace with God for God is within. And, if you are at war with yourself, you cannot be within God's peace.

Everyone these days looks at the 'keep the Sabbath' idea as though it were a gift to God. And yet it is God's gift to humanity that God has said, "Take the day off. Focus on yourself. Be mindful of the divinity within." Allow God's holy joy to be expressed in your life. Do not drive yourself so constantly that you lose touch with your own inner core of Light.

Passage 28

Jesus said, "I stood in the midst of the world, and I appeared to them in the flesh. I found them all drunk; I did not find any of them thirsting. And my soul was pained for the sons of men because they are blind in their heart, and they do not see that they came empty into the world; they seek to go out of the world empty. However, they are drunk. When they have shaken off their wine, then they shall repent."

I came into the world and stood before humanity in the flesh and they did not see the wonder of it. They were as those who are in a drunken stupor, their senses dull, unawakened. They did not thirst for knowledge or experience. They were sated with drink, with the illusion. They did not seek more.

So, I saw their indifference to me and I thought, how sad for them. For, I had come to bring a great gift. To bring them something that – if I didn't bring it – would take them a long time to find on their own. Maybe all eternity. And, here I am, holding out the gift of my own life – and by that I do not meant simply the sacrifice of the crucifixion – but my life as a human being. And, they don't know or care. How very sad for them. It is the greatest gift anyone could have asked to receive, and they don't recognize it. They don't know it. They do not know their own emptiness. They don't know what they are missing; they are caught up in the illusion and don't even see there is more.

So, they live their lives on the surface. And, it was

so sad to see them like that – it is still sad today to see people like that. When I speak of shaking off their drunkenness, to awaken, it is shaking off the dullness of the inner senses. It is shaking off the numbness of the mind. It is shaking off the illusion that the material world is all there is. The material world is only part of what adds flavor to the human experience. Yet, it is the surface dressing and people who drink deeply from only the surface get drunk on the illusion.

Rise up humanity! Learn to see beyond illusion and you will find the core of what Is.

Passage 29

Jesus said, "If the flesh exists because of spirit, it is a miracle, but if spirit (exists) because of the body, it is a miracle of miracles. But I marvel at how this great wealth established itself in this poverty."

If the body exists because of spirit, it is a miracle. What is a miracle? It is an act of God! If the body exists at the prompting of spirit, it is an act of God. A miracle. But, if the spirit exists because of the body, that would be a miracle of miracles indeed, for the body is not a god. And sometimes I marvel at how this wealth of spirit exists in such poverty, in such emptiness.

On this planet you have the various kingdoms: the mineral, the plant, the animal and then humanity. You might call mankind the higher self of the humanity kingdom. Humanity is God's creation through which God's Light and loving creative intent flow into mankind.

When we breathed spirit into the pre-human creature who then became newly human, there was already an animal instinct program established, of killing for food as well as harvesting for food – eating fruits and vegetables and leaves and roots. So, the 'choice' program was already in place, but the choices were based on evolutionary choices – pragmatic choices and not on 'right and wrong' or 'do and don't.'

When we breathed the spirit into the newly human, we also began to guide him. We put thoughts in his mind that said, "It is not good to kill your brother," and "It's not good to kill one's family," and "It's not good to destroy just for the sake of destruction." And when he became somewhat more sophisticated intellectually, then we said, "There is a being more powerful than you called 'God.' God doesn't want you to kill other people. You mess with God, you are liable to feel God's punishment." The God concept that we showed this primitive human was much like a bigger, stronger human. A superhuman is called God. So, it's been a step-by-step process.

If you look at parts of the world today, there are many who have not progressed. They have become more sophisticated intellectually, and there are nations that are 'civilized,' but even those that have become more sophisticated, many of them live in the same conditions that were prevalent when I walked the earth.

Yet, sometimes I marvel at how the God Light shines in even the most negative, the most primitive of humanity. In him, who has not yet discovered it himself. In her, who is a long way from seeing herself even as truly human, much less a god. In those who are still so close to their animal progenitors, the physical animal creatures from whom they evolved. I look at it and I say it is a supreme miracle that we have indeed managed to affix the spirit, the wealth, the light into these primitive vessels. And you know, the wonder is not that so many failed to affix, but that so many succeeded.

Passage 30

Jesus said, "Where there are three Gods, they are Gods; where there are two or one, I am with him."

I haven't the faintest idea where they got that. I'm trying to think of what I might have said that could have been translated in this way. However, my interpretation is that I am with every God who is truly God, for in the beginning, we were One. And, no matter how many divisions you make of it, we are still One. If there are two Gods or one, I am a part of it.

I am with every God. I am with every bit of God's own Light including that part which is vested or seeded in humanity. You have often heard me say that the Christ consciousness is within every human heart, even unawakened though it may be in by far the greater number of them. I am with you, each and every one. I am with every God, for there can be no God without God-ness and I am within it.

Remember what I have said that the idea of God, as presented to the early human, was rather like a human with super powers, and with human motivations like anger, love, desire, and human ego wanting to be acknowledged as the greatest God. So, the *concept* of Godhood has grown for humanity, as humanity's understanding of what Godhood is has also grown. But, it is also very true that in the old days, there were rival Gods for Yahweh. That is, there were those who wanted to be the greatest God of all. And, at some point, it was necessary for God's greatness to be demonstrated, so that you couldn't have just any one of the Gods setting up shop on every street corner of earth.

Yet, there is nothing wrong with seeing the many faces of God. There is nothing wrong with seeing God's Light in the Buddha, in Mohammed, or Shiva for indeed, it is truly vested there. There is nothing wrong with seeing God's Light in a human who is letting God's Light shine brightly through. There is nothing wrong with seeing God's Light in everyone and everything, or in recognizing that it shines more brightly in some people and in some places than in others.

We look at the American Indians for example, who see God in all life. Who see gods in the wolf, or the spider, or what have you. And each God-being, each supernatural being has a different personality and a different flavor, and plays a particular role in interaction with humanity.

Look at the Norse mythology and we see Loki, the trickster god who is much like Coyote to American Indians, and much like Ho-Toi (an expression of the laughing Buddha) – except that Ho-Toi is a bit more gentle in his 'tricking'!

Look also at the 'cargo cults' of the south Pacific. To the primitive tribesmen there, beings who flew in strange machines were supernatural and they had no words other than 'God' to call them. And, the Gods sent them cargo – good things in these strange vessels. After the war when the cargo gods stopped coming, the natives built airplanes out of straw to try to entice the gods to come again with their miraculous cargo.

To a Neanderthal man, you would have seemed divine. So, the concept of Godhood is basically a human one. We know who we are! Do you think I need a name to call myself? I Am who I Am. The human is the one who draws the boundary line and considers himself or herself 'not god.'

Passage 31

Jesus said, "A prophet is not acceptable in his own village; a physician does not heal those who know him."

There is something inherently mysterious and seemingly more worthy of respect in the stranger. In my own village for instance, there were people – other boys – who stood with me by the wall and peed on the wall as was the custom in such communities. I guess when you stood in a line, pissing at the wall together, it's hard to think of that person next to you as being different, or special, or more gifted than you are.

There were people who remembered when I was a baby, and who remembered when I ran around playing games with the other boys. There were people who could say, "I knew your momma." That is what is meant by the phrase "familiarity breeds contempt." When you know someone well, you tend to take them for granted and you form a viewpoint of the person that is based on your own experience. So, it is hard for you to set aside your personal view of the individual and see him or her as something mysterious and great. If you do glimpse the greatness, it tends to be more troubling than if you see that same greatness in a stranger. For, you begin to ask yourself questions. Has he changed? Could I have somehow failed to notice this? What kind of a strange world is it that we live in? It is easier, more comfortable, to be in awe of the stranger.

As far as the physician goes, well, you know if you have a medical doctor in the family you have probably seen him or her angry. You have probably seen him do something frivolous. You have probably seen her from time to time make mistakes. Not only that, but it is hard for a physician to set aside his own view of the personality in his own family to treat them. Even today, physicians generally do not treat their own families. It is not customary and it is not wise, for there is that little bit of professional distancing between doctor and patient that is needed to bring out the best in both of them for the situation.

Passage 32

Jesus said, "A city they build and fortify upon a high mountain cannot fall, nor can it be hidden."

This relates to the two-sided coin of power. If you are powerful, it's hard to hide it. The fortress on the mountaintop will be seen by most people as unapproachable, untouchable, and perhaps as a place of refuge in time of trouble. But, for ambitious warlords, it will be a challenge and a target and they will come to try to tear it down.

The thing to remember is that the fortress within built on a solid foundation of wisdom, faith and strength cannot be destroyed from outside. Usurpers will have to find a climb over point. And, you see, someone whose Light shines brightly is like a fortress. There are people who come to shelter in the Light, especially in times of trouble. There are people who pass by on the road in the valley and look up to the hills and say, "It's good to know there's someone strong up there, and if a time of trouble comes, I will know where to go for help."

There are some people who say, "I want nothing to do with it. It frightens me to see someone so strong." And, there will be those who say, "Hmm. Looks like quite a challenge. I wonder how long it will take me to tear it down?"

Here again, it comes back to where you are coming from. The point is, everyone knows it's there and everyone reacts to it by his or her own choices.

Passage 33

Jesus said, "What you hear in your ear, preach in [other's] ear[s from] your housetops. For no one kindles a lamp and puts it under a basket, nor does he put it in a hidden place, but he sets it on a lampstand so everyone who comes in and goes out will see its light."

What you hear in your ear…that is, what you receive in the way of knowledge, go and share it with others. Preach it from the pulpit. What you have received, share it with others, for that's the way word gets around. You don't light a candle and then put a cover over it so it can't be seen. You put the light where everyone will see it as they pass by.

The word 'hear' also means, in this instance, what you feel to be true. What you have received. You can say, "I hear that," meaning, I receive it. Go about and share it with others. This has to do with the value of educating your community and humanity, and not being an isolationist, not guarding a nugget of information jealousy as though you are the only person who must have it.

Find the way that is comfortable for you to share. But, do not be confused here…some people might think I am referring to 'witnessing for God' in the manner encouraged by modern religions. Witnessing as it is often practiced, is just another way of being egotistical and preachy. If you truly want to share something, then let it be something you have truly received from God. Not something you have received from the preacher or minister. Most witnessing as it occurs today is a church's way of turning its members into an intrusive, evangelical force into other people's lives.

Think of that way as compared to the way described in the last sentence of this passage: put the light where everyone can see it as they pass by. What you do, the ways in which you let your Light shine, speak louder than any words you can use to talk about your experience. The Light of God is like a wondrous feast…lay it out for all to see, and those who are searching and hungry will join you.

Passage 34

Jesus said, "If a blind man leads a blind man, the two of them fall into a pit."

That is pretty straightforward! To put it another way, if a man who has no vision is lead by another who has no vision, they will both fall into big trouble. Yet, there are so many who are intellectually, morally and spiritually blind, who want to be leaders.

What it really means is: choose your teachers wisely. Don't follow someone just because he or she says, "Come on! I'll be the leader!" For, he or she may be flawed in their vision just as you may be flawed in yours. Look for a teacher who can see clearly, who has vision. How can you know? Well, maybe you are tired of climbing up out of yet another pit! It's time to make a change!

Look for that light that is put by the door, so everyone who goes in and comes out can see it. Look for someone you admire. And, when it comes right down to it, don't automatically declare yourself to be blind! For, sight has many meanings and the blindness I'm speaking of here is metaphorical.

Maybe you aren't blind; maybe you don't need a leader. Maybe you don't need someone to follow. Maybe you have as much sight as the next person. Maybe you can say to God, "I am ready for my eyes to be open, now. Please heal my sight."

Feel your way along. Haven't we all done that? When I was a human, and had to walk at night, I didn't always light a candle. I felt my way along! We've all felt our way along in some situations. Choose your leaders wisely, just as you would choose your steps wisely on an unfamiliar path.

You can always choose to follow me. I have proven my worthiness as a leader. You can let my Light illuminate your path.

Passage 35

Jesus said, "It is impossible for one to enter the house of the strong man and rob it violently, unless he binds his hands; then he shall pillage his house."

You can't go into a strong household intending to rob it blind when you know you are up against an opponent stronger than you are. The direct frontal assault doesn't work. You will have to find a way to neutralize the householder.

The message here is really for the strong one rather than the thief. It says, "Don't take your strength for granted and allow someone to bind your hands. Don't allow yourself to get so bogged down through buying into other people's scenarios that they call you into doing what they want."

Fear is very much a binding. Sometimes control is taken by manipulation rather than direct force. Sometimes those who take control do it over a long period of time. They bide their time and hold their agendas close over many lifetimes, and then when they see the object of their desire has come to a weak point, they bring out the hidden power and take control. Physically, they wait until you are born into a position where fighting back is very difficult.

The main point here is to explain that the verse is intended to reach the householder rather than the thief, and to say to the householder, "Do not allow someone to bind your hands. Do not give your strength away. Do not give your power away." For, when you do this, the unworthy one can come in and do what he or she wants in your life.

Passage 36

Jesus said, "Do not be anxious from morning to evening and from evening to morning about what you will put on yourselves."

This passage speaks of scarcity consciousness. It speaks of worrying about what you will wear, where you will live. It speaks of getting so caught up in the worry that you become paralyzed.

In those days, a great many people wore their wealth, for there were few safe places a person of modest means could leave his or her possessions and truly know they were safe. They wore, for instance, not only jewelry that was made of gold and silver, but they would sew coins and precious objects into their garments.

So, the wealth was worn upon the person. And, the passage means don't worry about your wealth – the thought itself can become paralyzing. It really wasn't intended as a verse against vanity, although some people have taken it to be so. It was intended as a verse about scarcity consciousness as it is now called.

The problem with scarcity consciousness is that it tends to attract the very thing the person fears – loss of something valued. Fear is an energy. And, like any energy it flows out from a person and seeks to find the thing it is most like – itself. It's the law of attraction. There are volumes and volumes written on what is called 'the power of positive thinking.' Fear of loss is just the other side of the coin, which is, you might say, 'the power of negative thinking.' In either case, you tend to experience that which you put your focus on.

Passage 37

His disciples said, "On what day will you be revealed to us and on what day will we see you?" Jesus said, "When you undress without being ashamed, and you take your clothes and put them under your feet as little children and tramp on them, then you will see the Son of the Living (One) and you will not fear."

My companions said to me, "You've been talking about yourself and the wonders of who you are." And, it was true. I came to say, "Look, I can do these things." And, of course, the rest of the message was that so can you, when the time is right. But, they were saying, "When are you going to reveal yourself to us? When are you going to show yourself so clearly that we can have no doubt?"

In the world today, there are many people who will go to a healer or psychic and say, "Prove it to me." It's like that popular line from Jesus Christ Superstar: Prove that you are what you say you are. So, in effect, my companions were saying 'prove it to me.' And I said, "When you have no need of concealment, no need to clothe your nakedness – I did not mean the nakedness of the body – but, when you have no need to conceal who you are and you can throw off the posturing and the images of yourself that you put before others, when you can throw off these illusions and they are of so little importance to you that you would trample them underfoot as a child does a discarded garment, then I won't have to do anything. You will see me as I Am, for *you* will have been changed."

You will see me as I Am and you will not be afraid. You will have proven it to yourself.

Happily there are a great many, who, even if they do not understand the intellectual concepts of what I tried to teach, they do understand it emotionally and intuitively. The energy feels right to them. They literally see the Light and follow it.

You know, when I was Jesus, the man, I didn't look 2000 years ahead. I looked two hours or two days or two weeks or two months or two years ahead, and tried to prepare my followers, my dearest companions, for the work that they would do in my name. And when I became, once more, not just Isa the man, but the risen Christ, then all time was mine once more and I have not divided it into centuries or millennia. I have only watched the tapestry being woven. And, it is turning out to be beautiful. For all the ugliness, there is also great beauty in it.

Passage 38

Jesus said, "Many times you desired to hear these words which I say to you and you have no one else from whom to hear them. There will be days when you will seek me, and you will not find me."

Often you have wanted me to tell you something wise and wonderful that you cannot hear from anyone else. Often you have wanted me to give you something special to think about. Isn't it interesting that people come to me, even today, with the same interests and intent? It pleases me that people see the value in what I have to say and want to hear more of it. And, when I said to them, "Sometimes you will seek me and not find me," that is still true today, for sometimes people reach out to me wanting something wise and wonderful, miraculous or spectacular, and they don't get what they thought they were coming for.

Sometimes what I have to give is misunderstood or simply not understood, or sometimes people think they are coming to me and yet their hearts are not open to hear what I have to say. So, this lack of openness, this closedness, is like a barrier between us, and they seek but do not find me.

Yet, if you keep seeking, sooner or later you will find it. So, the saying, "Seek and you will find," is our way of saying, "We hear you and we will respond." It is true; when people come and ask us for conversation, for ideas, for sayings, we are glad to oblige.

The key point here is that when people seek me and want to hear my words, they are specifically looking for something they won't get somewhere else. They are looking for something wiser and more wonderful, or as you know, sometimes just saying the same thing in a little bit different way can bring insight.

Passage 39

Jesus said, "The Pharisees and the Scribes took the keys of knowledge; they hid them. They did not enter, and they did not allow to enter those who wanted to enter. But you be wiser than serpents and as innocent as doves."

The Pharisees and the scribes took the keys of knowledge and hid them. It was as though they regarded education and information as their personal property. Instead of sharing it with the people, they used it to brag about how smart they were, what thinkers and what keepers of the keys of knowledge they were.

Yet, because they kept the keys of knowledge away from the people, they did not enter into truer, deeper knowledge or wisdom. For, had they been more knowledgeable and more wise, they would have seen that there was greater advantage in sharing information than in withholding it. So, when I said to my followers, "You must be as shrewd as snakes and as innocent as doves," I was saying, "Be alert. Don't let anyone put anything over on you. Don't buy this exclusivity that the Pharisees and scribes are selling. Don't buy the idea that knowledge is unavailable to you. And yet, you must also be innocent in that when the information itself comes to you by whatever means, do not play the exclusivity game. Don't play the game of knowledge is power, of withholding power, withholding knowledge. Be innocent. Be outgoing. Be giving. Be sharing."

When you think of doves, you think of peace. But, there was more meaning in the phrase 'be innocent as doves.' We had a bit of a different word for it, and it meant to be as gentle, as sweet and as innocent as doves. As giving. As peaceful. But, also be as shrewd as a snake. Snakes are wisdom figures in the ancient literature (as you know, a snake was used to represent 'knowledge' in the Garden of Eden). To be as able to receive wisdom, to receive knowledge as a wise snake is said to be. And yet, be as innocent as a dove, as open and outgoing as a dove in sharing that knowledge.

The serpent was, you see, at the time this little allegorical story of the Garden of Eden was given, already a figure of knowledge. And of knowledge – well, it was still believed in those times that knowledge could be dangerous. Even now we say a little knowledge is a dangerous thing. It is true that knowledge without wisdom does have a tendency to be misused. So, knowledge in and of itself, although it is powerful, knowledge does not give character to the power. It can be powerfully negatively used or powerfully positively used.

Look at how the tabloid publications ferret out people's secrets and use them, in our view, negatively, to harm or embarrass. And, then again, look at how positively knowledge is used when there is some brilliant discovery that everyone can share, or when some deep philosophical insight comes to light that everyone can benefit from.

The Tree of Knowledge in the Garden of Eden represented self-responsibility, free will. It was – allegorically – the point at which the pre-human animal became human. It was a loss of innocence. Humanity gained choices. The story is an allegory for the first choice. Wise or unwise, it makes no difference. It was simply the first choice. Up until then, in the words of the allegory, God did all their thinking for them. It was the introduction of negative opportunity, of temptation. The Luciferic energy was what was personified as the serpent, as the tempter in the Garden of Eden. It was (still is) simply the one who presented a choice. Up until then, there hadn't been any choice to make.

And Eve, who has taken the blame, if you will, for eating from the Tree of Knowledge, was cast in that role largely due to society's view of females in the time the allegory was created. You must remember that women were viewed as beings of lesser spirituality in those times.

Knowledge was a way to control the masses. Knowledge was one of the most carefully guarded commodities. Even today, there is what is called proprietary information and copyrighted information. And in some cases, that is quite appropriate. But, you don't actually gain any ground by hoarding knowledge. You gain by sharing it, perhaps selectively, perhaps even by selling it when it is proprietary like a technique or product you have developed. But, if you just write it all down and lock it away, then nothing comes of it.

So, I was telling them to absorb knowledge, to become wise and share it freely. Share it in gentle innocence.

Passage 40

*Jesus said, "A vine was planted without the Father and it
has not strengthened; it will be pulled up by its roots (and)
it will rot."*

The grapevine is a symbol of life. Where the seeds
of life are sown, where the vine is planted too far from
sustenance, it cannot flourish and will die and be pulled up
and cast aside. When you plant a vine or a shrub, you must
plant it in an appropriate place and you must nurture it for a
time. The people of the times in which I was speaking
were farmers and they knew a lot about cultivating
grapevines. They knew if you just went out and planted a
vine any old place and did not go back and water it, it
would die. It would be pulled up. If you planted it too near
the roadway, when someone passed along it might catch on
the animal's hooves and be torn up.

These days, if you don't want the lawnmower to get
it, you have to build a little fence around it or put a flag on
it, or something. And, it was that kind of thing when I said
the vine planted too far from the Father can't flourish, and
will die and be pulled up. The father here being the
caregiver, the protector.

Since the grapevine is allegorical of life, a life that
attempts to be lived too far from the Light, the source of
wisdom, the source of connection to the cosmos, cannot
flourish. It takes the power of the giver of life. It takes the
protection of the giver of life to nourish and nurture a life.

The part about being pulled up means, in this case,
that the raw energy of the life, instead of being passed on

from generation to generation reincarnated, would simply be composted. It would go back to the raw energy pool. By the law of conservation of energy, nothing is ever truly lost; things only change form. But, that doesn't specify how they change.

Lives that are not worth continuing are discarded. If there are people who willfully choose not to progress on the path of spiritual growth, those who have continually made the choice not to make any progress, and this choice is habitually ingrained in them over many lifetimes, then there is no reason to believe that they will benefit from future incarnations, for it would simply be more of same. So, they are not reincarnated, they are reabsorbed into the All in a different way, at a different level, for we are all part of the All – we are all absorbed in it. The difference is that these ones are not aware – they do not achieve the bliss of Oneness – nirvana. But, it is re-entry into the All.

It's important to remember that everyone has played a negative role or made negative choices at some time. We don't hold that against them. It is the habitual negative choice – well, think of the definition of a sociopath. A sociopath has no empathy for anyone else, does not value the feelings of any other creature, whether human, animal or insect. The sociopath is entirely self-focused. For that person, the self has become the all and that individual cannot see beyond the self to any other form of all. When that ultimate self-absorption has become ingrained so that it is simply repeated lifetime after lifetime, and in spite of the counseling that occurs between lifetimes, then it is not worthy of being replicated. What would be the point?

Most of the people who behave negatively, even those who behave negatively on a grand scale, are simply playing the negative role for experience, for balance, for it being appropriate at that particular moment, and it is not presumed or supposed that they will continue in one negative lifetime after another. It is the habitual negative choice with no interest in any other choice but the selfish one, the negative one that causes the problem.

Passage 41

Jesus said, "He who has in his hand, it shall be given to him; and he who does not have, even the little he has shall be taken away from him."

There are other interpretations, other versions of this saying in the other gospels. This of course refers to a well-known story in the Bible. It is about the master who went away on a journey. He gave to each of his servants one talent – one unit of money. One of the servants, while the master was gone, lost it, and another buried it to keep it safe, and the third took it out and made more money with it.

So, the one who had lost it didn't get any points. The one who had buried it also didn't get any points because he just didn't work it. But, the one who had made money with it was rewarded. To him who had much was given more.

They used the word 'talent,' which was a monetary unit, in that little parable as a play on words having to do with one's innate talents, or abilities. What we are saying here is, to someone who has made much of his resources, who has increased his spiritual wealth, to him more will be added – it will be given. To the one who has done nothing to improve himself, he will find himself having less and less, for if he doesn't care enough about himself to make an effort, then in effect, God says, "Well, he's going to have to learn on his own. I won't continue to bail him out. I'll bring his lessons to him even faster."

This verse was also intended to send the message that God helps those who help themselves. To one who has much and grows much, this one will receive encouragement and assistance. God respects and treasures the rightful audacity of someone who claims his power or her power. Claiming your power is a goodly thing – a Godly thing – and it is good in God's eyes.

Passage 42

Jesus said, "Be wanderers."

This passage has also been interpreted to say, "Be passersby." A passerby is an observer. A passerby is someone who does not take root but who keeps moving. To be a passerby in that time meant not settling down in a village, not taking on one role – life's role – and living it until the end of the incarnation. But it was to keep wandering. Keep moving on the path of life. Keep moving on the path of spiritual growth. Continue to experience new things. Don't allow yourself to become crystallized.

There are all sorts of modern phrases that have this kind of a ring. Keep on truckin'. Keep on keeping on. Keep moving. And even Satchel Paige's, "Don't look back. Something might be gaining on you." The point is to continue to move, to grow, to learn.

What is the alternative to being a passerby? It is to be passed by. It is to be sessile. To be just sitting there and letting life pass you by.

Let us take someone whose life in those days and times was very narrowly limited – let's say a mother with very small children who had all the duties of taking care of her home and family in a primitive time. It was constant work, and a constant struggle for basic necessities. Yet, even she could be a passerby. She could be moving through life observing the workings of her home and family, noticing how her children were growing up, responding to her growing up children differently according to their age groups. She could be living a life of growth, even in the narrowness of her focus and her duties. She could notice what is going on around her, or as she goes through the village, she could exercise a bit of detachment by not getting caught up in the neighbor's struggles, but keeping her focus on her own path.

When you are focused on your own path, it does mean you will pass some other things by. So, there are several ways of interpreting this that are all correct. Be passersby also means keep following your own path. Don't stop off and involve yourself in someone else's path. You can learn from them, you can observe, and it may even be part of your path to help them. But, keep your focus on your own concerns, your own chosen path.

If you follow your path, you will pass things and people by. I was also speaking specifically to my twelve friends and companions. I was talking to them about how I envisioned their roles in the days to come after I had left them. I did ask them to go out into the world and help spread my teaching. In doing this, I did say, "I see you as travelers, not becoming absorbed and staying in one place. Carrying the teaching you have to offer to many communities. If you do this, you will be passersby; you will be wanderers. You won't get absorbed in every last little detail. You will teach the teachers and heal the healers. You won't try to be all things to all people. There are problems that you will observe along the way and you will pass them by. For, it is not appropriate for you to attempt to solve every problem or to participate in every situation."

Be willing to keep moving. Keep going on your path and you will pass by much of the world. If you are also growing fast, then you are going to be moving on your path faster than a lot of other people are moving on their paths.

You know how much you've been through, in letting go of people who could not keep pace with you. I also meant that. Pass by that which is no longer appropriate for you. Pass by those people in whose interaction you can no longer play the role they need, and in whose interaction with you, they can no longer play the role you need. Don't be afraid to say goodbye and move on.

110

Passage 43

His disciples said to him, "Who are you that you say these things to us?" "By what I say to you, you do not know who I am, but you have become as the Jews. They love the tree, they hate its fruit; they love the fruit, they hate the tree."

Well, they did say from time to time, "Who are you to say these things to us?" I must confess, they weren't being confrontational as in saying, "Who do you think you are?" Instead they were asking, "Who *are you* to be saying this to us?" Sometimes even now when a channel or a teacher says something that really touches the listener, the listener will pause and think, "Who are you, that you have said this to me?"

Listeners may even say, "Who are you channeling that has said this to us? Where did that come from? Who are you?" Well, the answer of course is you are a part of God's own Light. That was the answer for me. I am the Light of God to say these things to you. And I am a bridge as it were between God and humanity to bring Godly wisdom into words that you can hear, and at least some of you can absorb.

You do not know who I am by what I say to you. So, I was saying to them, "You have not recognized the power in my words. You have not seen the power behind the words. You have only glimpsed it from time to time. You do not hear who I am, the Light of God in the words I say. You have become like the Jewish people, accustomed to God's presence in your life and thoughts, and taking it somewhat for granted."

The Jewish people by that time had known they were the chosen people of Yahweh. This teaching had been handed down for quite some time, and it had become so familiar that they took it for granted. And some of them loved the roots of the tree, that is, the roots of their tradition, but didn't like the way the traditions were manifesting in the day and time in which they lived. In other words, they were historians who respected and treasured the energy, the message, the feeling of the roots of their faith. Yet, they did not bring it into the present and live it in the present.

Others appreciated the fruit of the tree, that is, the benefits that came to them from their religion, from their traditions, yet they had no knowledge of or real interest in how their traditions of faith had come into being. They were just living in the Now. There's much to be said for living in the Now. There's much to be said for having an appreciation of history, but I would say the best is a balance of the two. A balance is if you can look at the tree of knowledge – in this case the knowledge of the Jewish religion – and see the beauty of the roots of how it began and how it grew, and at the same time have a genuine appreciation for the rest of the tree up to and including the fruit that it bears.

It's important to be able to look at the Jewish tradition and religion today, and see the good in it. See the unique gifts that people of Jewish heritage have brought forth into the world and continue to bring forth into the world today. For a religion – any religion – is a pattern of thinking, a pattern of living, a way of life to those who follow it. The pattern of thinking, the pattern of living one layer on another, generation after generation, strengthens and expands certain abilities. It is like a narrowing of focus, yes? And it is part of the beauty and wonder of the

112

earth that these different trees of faith, these different ways of life bring forth slightly different fruit.

You might look at Judaism, Islam and Christianity as being different varieties of apple tree. They are all apple trees, for they all worship the one God – Yahweh, Allah, Jehovah – it is One and it is acknowledged to be the same among the three of them. They all believe there is but one God and they all come from that monotheistic specific God root. Yet, the fruit of each of them looks a little different and tastes a little different from the other two varieties of apple.

When you look at all these different kinds of apples, you may have a favorite variety of apple. But, they are still all apples. If you can appreciate the root, the history of the apple, and still also appreciate the fruit of the particular variety of apple tree that is your preference, then you are honoring the tradition, the history and the Now. So, you see how this relates to the verse?

Let's say you are in the produce section of a grocery store and you are picking up apples and putting them in your cart. Do you attack the person next to you who is buying a different kind of apple? Do you feel threatened because that person is making a different choice? Do you feel bound to put your apples back and choose the ones the other person is buying instead? Do you feel guilty – or superior – because you have chosen a different kind of apple? Do you feel the need to go to the store manager and demand that he or she stop carrying any other type of apple other than the kind you buy? Do you feel a need to witness about the merits of your kind of apple to convince the other person to change their selection?

All this seems silly, doesn't it? You don't look at each other and say, "Oooh. How could you choose a Winesap instead of a Granny Smith?" Yet, what makes you think people's choices about religion are any different?

Look around. There's a lot of silliness in the world today simply because people like different varieties of apple trees.

Respect the differences and enjoy the variety. That is the wonder of the earth. Respect the fruit of diversity that the trees in God's garden have borne.

Passage 44

Jesus said, "One who blasphemes the Father, it will be forgiven him, and one who blasphemes the son, it will be forgiven him, but one who blasphemes the Holy Spirit, it will not be forgiven him, either on earth or in Heaven."

There are many ways of looking at God the Father. The way of seeing God in the mind's eye in the time in which this was written, was very anthropomorphic, was very human-like and father-like. And, all children can go through phases where they say, "I hate you, father," or "He's no good," and be forgiven, for it is a natural thing sometimes to have a conflict with one's father. It is also a very natural thing to feel as a human sometimes, that one has a conflict with one's God, because remember, we are talking about the human concept of God, which is human-like.

Even today, there may be someone who prays to me, "Please Jesus, do this for me," or "Please Jesus get me out of this mess," or even, "Oh, Lord, won't you buy me a Mercedes Benz," and who prays, and prays and prays, and I don't give the answer he or she wants. Sometimes the person will say, "Damn you. I don't believe in you," or "There's nothing to this Jesus myth." It's rather like a child who stomps his or her foot in a temper tantrum. "Give it to me, or else!" Give it to me – prove it to me – or I won't believe in you. And, like the wise father or elder brother, we forgive the human-child for the temper.

But, someone who says there's no such thing as a holy spirit – notice I said 'a' holy spirit rather than 'the' holy spirit – is, in effect, denying all Gods everywhere for all times, including the God within. It is that kind of a dark night of the soul that is not easily forgiven, such as, "Oh, yes, I forgive you. I know you didn't mean it." It is a more serious matter, not in terms of being condemned for it, but meaning that repentance is necessary. Remember that the word 'repent' means to think again. So, re-thinking is called for when one denies or blasphemes against the holy spirit, who is the principle, the personification of spiritual energy.

To deny the existence of spirit...well, to deny all religions is OK, but to deny all spirituality, to say there is nothing there, is not easily forgiven. It is an issue that needs to be dealt with. Now, most people who are atheists aren't really atheistic, that is, without God; they mostly just don't want to have to think about it. They are usually agnostic – it just means they don't know. But, those few who deny the existence of any god, of any spirit, yes, they have to repent rather than simply being forgiven.

Sometimes, when these people see the evidence, they repent, they re-think pretty darn fast. But, if they don't 'see the light' when the evidence is before them, then they struggle in darkness for as long as it takes them to think again, to repent. That is the meaning of purgatory in the Roman Catholic Church. It is the place between this life and heaven or hell. It is not hell; it is not heaven. It is a place for repentance, for re-thinking, for counseling.

Many people think of forgiveness as God forgiving them when they do something wrong, but it's more of a case of reaching understanding within and forgiving themselves. To forgive is to give up the worry of it, the obsessing over it. To stop making an issue of it. And, forgiveness doesn't necessarily require repentance because sometimes you can be forgiving without having to think about it. Without thinking things over, you know instinctively, "I was angry and spoke rashly. I didn't mean it and everyone knows it."

The point is that simple forgiveness is not enough in some cases. The situation may require repentance – a re-thinking that leads to spiritual growth.

Passage 45

Jesus said, "They do not pick grapes from among thorns, nor do they gather figs from among camel's thistles; they do not give fruit. F[or a go]od man brings forth good fr[om] his treasure; a b[ad] man brings forth evil from his evil treasure in his heart, and he speaks evil. For out of the abundance of his heart, he brings forth evil."

It is said so many different ways. By their fruits, ye shall know them. That was the preliminary to this verse. A good person brings forth good fruit. When I first began speaking through this channel, and people said, "How do we know if it's real or not?" we would say, "By their fruits ye shall know them." If it is good, then it is good. If it is not good, then it is not good. And, it is up to the listener to make that determination.

By now you know what is right and what is wrong. You know what is good and what is evil. Even by the time in which I spoke, good had been defined, and evil had been defined. There were the Ten Commandments, that code of behavior that was given at a time in which it was very much needed to give people guidelines to live by. Keeping those commandments was good. Breaking those commandments was considered bad, or evil. If you had someone who kept killing people, kept murdering, obviously this was an evil tree that brought forth evil fruit. Remember that the tree is the symbol of life and evil life brings forth evil fruit or evil deeds. A good tree brings forth good fruit or good deeds.

You don't harvest grapes off a thorn bush and you don't pick figs off a thistle. Do not expect good fruit from an inappropriate source. There is one of those little fables that speaks of a young girl who saw a rattlesnake when she was walking along a path one cold day. She recognized that it was dying, because it was cold. She spoke to the snake and it said, "Help me, I'm cold." And she said, "If I help you, you're a snake, you might bite me." The snake replied, "Oh, no. I'll be so grateful if you help me that I wouldn't bite you." So, she picked the snake up and put it inside her coat to warm it. And when it got warm, it bit her. She was horrified and said, "But you said you wouldn't bite me!" The snake said, "You knew I was a snake when you picked me up. You knew what I was. I was just being me."

Think about people who go into a marriage relationship with say, an alcoholic. The statement that often accompanies the divorce goes something like, "You knew I was an alcoholic when you married me." It was unrealistic of the person to expect the marriage partner to be anything else. And, women who marry men thinking they can reform or transform them, are expecting to pick figs off the thistle plant.

Acknowledge the evil nature of the tree, the incarnation, and don't expect it to produce something out of character. If it produces some good for you, it is often unintentional. A tough, but very necessary, lesson on the path of life.

You see, the key here is in discerning which is the evil tree and which is the good one. By their fruits ye shall know them. It is when the tree bears fruit, that you are in a position to judge. For, when the tree is younger or out of season and is not bearing at that moment, then sometimes you are in the position of having to guess what this tree's fruit might be. You can go around and ask, "Excuse me, neighbor. You've lived here longer than I have. What kind of fruit did this tree have on it last year?" How did this person behave in a previous situation? What is his or her track record?

You can also watch and wait, and when the season has come for harvest, you can see for yourself what kind of fruit the tree bears. Its true nature will always be revealed.

Passage 46

Jesus said, "From Adam to John the Baptist, among those born of women, no one is greater than John the Baptist, so that his eyes…[text is uncertain]. But I said that whoever among you shall become as a child shall know the Kingdom, and he shall become higher than John."

From Adam to John the Baptist…throughout the history of humankind, from the beginning until the life of John the Baptist, there was never such a Light-filled being as he. The averting the eyes refers to the degree to which his Light was shining. His Light was shining so brightly that others couldn't stand to see it clearly and would have to look away. Metaphorically, he was such a good man.

John was a being of Light, and the human side of him, the passion, was expressed in a different way. He was capable of being very firm, and so people sometimes said he was angry when it wasn't really anger; it was sheer, raw power. They didn't know any other way to express their response to it other than to say he was angry.

He was very powerful and has not been given his due by many who have remembered my life and his role in it, for he was more of a teacher to me than has been acknowledged. He helped me when I was young, to balance the power, and then for a time we separated, so that when I came back a grown man, he saw me anew and he saw my power. But, in this verse, I am speaking of the teacher I knew and loved whose gifts were very Light filled, very generous. He was unlike other men.

The verse goes on to say that whoever becomes as a little child will know the kingdom. I meant that, as human beings, you don't have to be filled with God's Light in the way that John was, in the way that I am, to be received into the kingdom of heaven. Into the company of the Light. You only need to have the good-hearted innocence of a child. That is the meaning of grace as opposed to works.

If I had come only to say, "Here is perfection," and had left the message that said you have to be as good as I am to get in, that would have been a pretty depressing message. In the same way, if I had said all these glowing things about how brightly John's Light shines, and then had said you have to be as good as John to get in, that would have been a discouraging thing for me to say to them. So, after I talked about how wonderful he was and how much I respected him, I then said, in effect, "Don't worry, you don't have to be like John to make the grade. You just have to have the good-hearted innocence and trust in God that a child has."

Passage 47

Jesus said, "A man cannot mount two horses; he cannot stretch two bows. A servant cannot serve two masters; either he will honor the one and the other he will scorn...No man drinks old wine and right away wants to drink new wine; and they do not put new wine into old wineskin lest they tear, and they do not put old wine into new wineskin lest it spoil it. They do not sew an old patch on a new garment, because there will be a tear."

A person cannot ride two horses or bend two bows, which means that if your focus is split, you can't do them both equal justice. Trying to do too many things at once, especially if they are diametrically opposed, just doesn't work. Duality, such as we have on this planet, is about choice. And riding two horses or bending two bows is about avoiding choice. Trying to do both and not having to choose.

All too often these days, when people are seeking a win/win solution, they will try to please everyone. They will try to avoid making a choice. They will temporize and theorize and try to have everything just to avoid making a choice. There is nothing wrong with trying for a win/win solution, make no mistake; however, when it isn't possible, you must make a decision and sometimes those choices are hard. Ultimately, you have to approach it from the point of view of which side has the better claim.

When it speaks of a man not being able to serve two masters, it speaks of humanity's capacity for, in effect, playing favorites. If you think about a secretary in an office pool who has to type reports for several bosses, this is a difficult thing because there is the human tendency to like or appreciate one boss more than the others. In these sophisticated times, of course, there are rules about this and it can be done. But, in the times in which I spoke, it was impractical to think in terms of someone working half time for two masters, because a servant was expected to be deeply invested in his master's affairs, and it was a full time job to work for any one master. He would short change one if he worked for two. He would favor one if he tried to work for two. It is better to have a clear focus on one task unless you genuinely have surplus time and energy.

Stop and think about the way people in that day and time did not have surplus time and energy. Today, you can serve two masters, so to speak, by having a job and a hobby. You can have a vocation and an avocation. You can have more than one priority and your time can be divided because you have leisure time. In those days, people didn't have the extra time and energy.

This passage also speaks of how one who has tasted aged wine will have a more sophisticated palate, and will be less likely to appreciate new wine, which has not had the benefit of aging. This verse also says one does not put new wine into an old skin, less the skin might break, nor does one put old wine into a new skin less the wine might spoil. This speaks of the different enzymes and chemical compositions in old wine and new wine. One should appreciate the old wine for its having aged, and treat it accordingly. One should appreciate the new wine for its vigor and youthful potential, and treat it accordingly. In other words, one should make appropriate decisions.

You follow a flow pattern that is appropriate to the circumstances of the materials you are working with. In working with humans that we are teaching, we follow a flow pattern that is appropriate for the material, the human material we are working with. We do not take someone who is old and wise and try to force them to ride roller blades or some such. And, we do not expect the young and vigorous to behave the way a wise elder would behave. We follow the flow pattern of the material we have to work with, and we seek to provide or maintain the resources that are appropriate to that growth stage.

You have heard us often say that you don't parent a two-year-old the same way you parent a grad student, and you don't parent a grad student the same way you parent a two-year-old. The principle here is the same. It means everything should be evaluated and used within its own context. When you break the flow, contextually, you set up opportunities for discord and failure.

There is that old saying, "Don't change horses in the middle of the stream." And, quite often, it means don't change leadership at a critical juncture in a successful project. You know this from business. There are companies that just keep moving their executives around for the sake of movement, and every time they do, something is lost. So, there is value in maintaining contextual flow.

In my time, things changed very slowly, so that to stay in context, to come to completion of a cycle, was a long process. Today, things move quickly and to stay in context may mean staying with it for only a short while before the cycle turns and a new context is established. The danger today is you may miss the moment where the context changes. You see, if you put the old context into a new container, the new container may sour the mellowness of the old context. You don't take a forward looking concept and try to push it into the past, and you don't take a past concept that has stopped working and try to push it into the future.

Regarding the old patch on a new garment theme, typically in those days, we wore cloth until we wore it out. Patches were made from old, outworn garments. The patch would have come from cloth that had already been used to the point that its strength was greatly diminished. So, if you put an old patch on a new garment, then the old cloth was not equal to the strength of the new cloth. The same can be said of using old concepts to plug holes in the fabric of new ideas or systems. The patches will create weak points and will not have the same duration as the fabric around it.

Passage 48

Jesus said, "If two make peace between themselves in the same house, they shall say to the mountain, 'Move away,' and it will be moved."

This speaks of the value of consensus and of reaching an agreement. There is power in reaching an agreement, a consensus. It is mutual enrollment. There is something about agreement that empowers all parties who are a part of it. And if you agree, you can move mountains.

I have also said at another time, "Where even two or three are gathered in my name, there I am also." Where there is agreement between two of you, the God Light, the force within is activated and you can move mountains. When you agree on a solution to a problem and put your minds to it together, you can move the blockages, the mountains as it were.

We have often spoken in our conversations about the power of conscious intent. What is an agreement? It is an expression of consciousness, of intent. If two people agree they are in love, it is a statement of conscious intent to be in love. They may say it prematurely, but if they say it with intention, then it becomes true and nothing can break it as long as they both intend it.

Two men who are merchants, if they agree on the conduct of business and what their goals are, it is a powerful thing. If even two are agreed on the business they are creating and conducting, they can 'move mountains.' Two children might be in agreement that they will build a sandcastle. They will move the mountain of sand because they are in agreement and they can build a powerful sandcastle.

There are people all over the world who are working at creating consensus. There are conservationists, there are ecologists, there are peacemakers, there are all sorts of focal points on which intention is consensually centered. And, intention is powerful. Consensus is powerful. That doesn't mean that your internal consensus is any less powerful than someone's external consensus. It simply means that one needs to be in agreement with people one is connected to, and one needs to be connected to people with whom one is in agreement.

Godhood is consensus. It is 'we are all One.' What greater statement of consensus is there?

Passage 49

Jesus said, "Blessed are the solitary and the chosen, because you will find the Kingdom; because you come from it, you will again go there."

Fortunate are those who are alone. Fortunate is one who stands apart from the consensus reality, the maya, the illusion that everyone else is enrolled in. You talked at supper about mothers in the South who taught their children not to be 'common.' This verse is saying, "Fortunate is one who is not common, who is alone." And, the implication is that this one is alone by choice, not hidden on a mountaintop or stuck in a cave and not knowing how to find the nearest village, but alone as an independent thinker.

Fortunate is the one who seeks the kingdom, who seeks the higher reality instead of just playing on the beach building sandcastles. There's nothing wrong with people building sandcastles, they are like children, but fortunate is the one who stands alone, an independent thinker seeking the kingdom. This one came from the kingdom and is on his or her way back there. Fortunate is the one who has correctly identified the purpose of human life. For, the purpose of human life is to independently seek the reunion, the return to Oneness.

Passage 50

Jesus said, "If they say to you, 'Where did you come from?'
say to them, 'We come from the light, where the light came
through itself. It stands [...] and reveals itself in their
image.'"

How 'New Age' that passage is. If they ask where
you come from, give them the answer that is the one true
answer for all of us now and forever. We come from the
Light. We come from that place where the Light
discovered itself. We come ultimately from the One
source, for there is ultimately only One source. How could
you come from anywhere else? The All-That-Is, is all that
is.

Then if they should say to you, "Well who are you?
Are you God then?" You can say, "I am a child of Light; I
am an expression of Light. I am who I am, and in my
individuality as you see it at this moment, in the expression
of Godhood that you see in me at this moment, I am God,
but I am not complete. I am not all of God."

In the time in which I spoke, it was very difficult for
them to understand how you could be God and not be all of
God. If I had said to them, "If someone asks you who you
are, say you're God." They would have said, "What if
people ask what God is?" Well, God is everything. God is
motion and rest. Einstein would have loved that.

We have come from the Light, from the place where
Light is, where Light established itself, and then created
itself in their image. That is what Edgar Cayce called the
First Cause. First you move from the singular to the plural,

and you also move from the non-sex linked gender term 'it' to 'their' which implies male/female or a combination of the two. The word 'their' is persona oriented, where 'it' is object oriented. So, it is moving from the concept of undifferentiated unified consciousness, to differentiated individual consciousness and the expression of selfhood. The 'selves' now become separate entities as compared to the One.

And, if they say, "The Light – is it you? Are you God?" Then you must say to them, "We are its children; we are the expression of Light and as such, are children of the living Father." This is to say we are of one family with the Light. We are the seeds that the Light has sown.

Passage 51

His disciples said to him, "When will be the rest of the dead and when will the new world come?" He said to them, "What you look for has come, but you do not know it."

When will the rest for the dead take place…in other words, when will the reward (for people thought of rest as reward since life was toil and hard work) be given? When they asked those questions, they were thinking as many people might think even now, today. When someone dies, do they get their heavenly rest immediately? Or, do they have to wait until the end of the world and they all rise back up together? There are plenty of religions that think it works that way.

It's the same kind of question that one might ask today. When will the dead receive their rest, and when will the new world begin? And, I said to them, "It is happening now. Those who have died are receiving their rest. For them, the new world has come." It is already happening – most people just don't know it. The communication doesn't come back from them to you, so you don't know what is happening with them, even now, as we speak.

Of course, there is a double meaning in this passage. For, they asked, "When will the new world come?" And, I said, "It has come and you don't know it." So, I was also speaking of myself for I brought the new world and they had not recognized it yet.

Both meanings are there, and I was thinking of both meanings as I spoke. There was actually more to what I said at the time. I did try to tell them that the dead are at rest and at peace. I did try to tell them that someone who has crossed through the gates of death, has crossed to a new beginning, a new life, a new world. But, it was very hard for them to grasp.

People today still have trouble with that one. Yet, more people can grasp it now, and in the general populace, most of them do believe that one's rest begins shortly after death. You see this if nothing else on the tombstones. Rest in Peace. Until We Meet Again.

Some people think the dead will have to wait until everybody gets there, and then they will rise up together to their rest. In any case, I hate to disillusion you, they don't wait for everyone to get there and then rise up. They rise as they receive the Light, the new life.

Passage 52

His followers said to him, "Twenty-four prophets have spoken in Israel, and they all spoke of you." He said to them, "You have disregarded the living one who is in your presence and have spoken of the dead."

They said to me, "Your coming was widely prophesized. All the prophets spoke of you." And I said, "The prophets who went before us have credibility with you, but that's not what makes me who I am." In effect, you shouldn't need the prophets to tell you who I am. You should be able to see it, to recognize it.

What if they had not spoken of me? My listeners were regarding the dead, the prophets who had gone before, more highly than they regarded me. And, I was thinking of John the Baptist as well, for they weren't speaking of him as a prophet. He is not listed as one of the prophets of Israel, yet of those who spoke of me, he spoke of me the most partly because it was in his time that my coming was most imminent. He was the forerunner, the one who came to prepare the way, and he told everyone that, yet he was not acknowledged as a prophet of Israel.

As you know, the Jewish people did not accept me for who and what I was. If they had accepted me as the Messiah, then it would have overturned all their traditions and they wouldn't have known where to begin. The Messiah they prayed for, they still pray for today. Each Jewish heart has his or her own vision of how that one shall come and how he shall appear and what it will mean to the world. Yet, it has been so long that they have been having these visions. At the feast of Passover every year, they say that next year, in Jerusalem, we will be restored to the closeness of the Promised Land. For, they still see Israel as the Promised Land.

If the Jews had accepted me as the Messiah, you know it was the priesthood that would have been displaced. It would have undermined their authority and the power would have passed to me. So, they couldn't let that happen. If the priests of Judaism had acknowledged me as the Messiah, they would have lost their power, for then they would have been compelled to bow before me and there was much fear. I would have abolished everything. After all, look at how it overturned the customs of those who did accept me.

It was known ahead of time that they would not all accept me. You know, the invitation has to be made even if it is refused. It was still the right thing to do to give them the opportunity to choose.

Yet, if the Jews had accepted me as the Messiah, then how would my ministry have gone beyond Judaism? For, in order to come to the Messiah of the Jewish people, others would have had to become Jews first. When official Judaism did not accept me, then it was easy for those of them who had accepted me to reach out and say we're not going to limit this to Jews. It was never my intention that I should be the captive of one religion only…even my own. Just as even now, it is not my intention to be the captive of any one religion – even my own – now that the religion is called Christianity.

Religion is a vessel of containment, so that the human has somewhere to put his relationship to God. Once the human knows that his relationship to God cannot be contained, then there is no more need for religion.

Passage 53

His disciples said to him, "Is circumcision profitable or not?" He said to them, "If it were profitable, their father would beget them circumcised (sic) from their mother. But the true circumcision in the Spirit has found complete usefulness."

Here we speak of the spiritual value of circumcision. The medical value of circumcision in warm climates is undeniable. But, that's not what we were talking about. When Abraham received the message from God to circumcise himself and his children, God knew there was medical benefit in it, and yet, that's really not what it was all about.

It was about setting themselves apart from other people, other populations. And, it was about a commitment to God, a dedication. If circumcision were essential, then indeed, the male children would have been born without a foreskin.

There's more to this, here. They were asking, in effect, when they said is circumcision useful, is do you have to be circumcised to enter the kingdom of heaven? And, of course, the answer is no. Many of my Godly friends weren't circumcised in their earthly lives. The Buddha laughs!

Again, the love and Light and wisdom, the joy of communion, the energy that I came to bring, does not depend on whether or not one is circumcised. And that's what I was trying to say.

The true circumcision in spirit speaks of the symbolic commitment, the symbolic change of tribe as Abraham began the new tribe. So, spiritually, when you make the energy commitment, you become part of a new spiritual tribe. It is a moving away from the animal toward the divine.

Passage 54

Jesus said, "Blessed are the poor, for yours is the Kingdom of Heaven."

Well, one interpretation on the surface level is the familiar phrase, "Pie in the sky, by and by when you die." It says to the poor, in effect, "Don't worry, you won't be poor in heaven." And, that was very important at the time. It does not speak against the rich, it only says that perhaps you have not found your fortune yet, but you are fortunate, for you will not be poor in heaven. It means don't worry; you have something to look forward to.

It is also a reference to karma, which says, in effect, you pay your dues. There is the implication that says someone who has had too easy a life, may have to pay his karmic dues in future lives, before he receives his reward. Why is this?

It is because the old law of karma was basically a teaching tool for behavior modification. Karma is actually a human concept. It is how the animal-human-god being learns. You see, if you learn your lesson on the first trip, you don't have to keep doing the same lesson again; you go on to another lesson. Let's take something less ambiguous than rich and poor. Let's take something clear-cut, such as kind or cruel.

Joe Schmoe, if he is in his first lifetime as a slave owner and the owner of beasts of many kind, and he treats his slaves and his livestock and those over whom he has power with fairness, with compassion, with kindness, then he gets the message without having to be a slave. Now, he may choose to incarnate as a slave for balance – to view the experience, you might say, from both sides of the fence. But, if Joe Schmoe has no compassion, if he is cruel rather than kind, if he does not show mercy to those who are under his power, then it's a pretty good bet that he has run up a karmic debt that will have to be paid.

Speaking of karma as a debt that must be paid, is no more than saying there is a lesson that he needs for his growth and he hasn't learned it yet. You can't go on to multiply 2,386 by 97 if you still haven't gotten the message that two plus two equals four.

You can't progress to the next grade level of soul development until you have passed the test in the current one. The good news is, the basic level at which you earn the right to choose your lessons is very modest. It is like kindergarten. And, there are several different ways of learning those lessons; one is by experience and that is karma; one is by observation and that is wisdom; and the other is by taking someone else's word for it, and that is grace.

The law of karma is strong. The law of wisdom is greater. The law of grace is the greatest of all.

Remember, there is a difference between wisdom and intelligence. Many have the intelligence to know what their options are, but do not have the wisdom to make good choices. Karma is the method in which people learn wisdom, through experience.

Passage 55

Jesus said, "He who does not hate his father and his mother cannot be my disciple and (he who) does not hate his brothers and his sisters and (does not) carry his cross in my way will not be worthy of me."

This passage is easily misunderstood. Whoever does not hate father and mother – here the word 'hate' is the problem in the misunderstanding. I didn't say hate. Whoever loves their father and mother, regarding them as flawless and cannot be independent of them, cannot follow me. Whoever cannot be independent of a brother and sister cannot follow me. Whoever is bound by tradition to the extent that he cannot remove himself, as a free thinker, from it, cannot follow me.

One who honors his father and his brother and the teachings of his father and siblings as primary, cannot become my disciple for only a free thinker, only someone who is willing to leave the traditions of his own family behind, can truly follow me.

Is it not so even today? Those who follow the teachings of the narrow church, simply out of loyalty for their family traditions, without an inquiring mind, without looking at it logically, not thinking upon it for themselves, cannot truly follow me. For I am a leader and people who follow blindly cannot be leaders. They can follow a church that professes to follow me, but they cannot follow *me* if they have no minds of their own.

Only someone with a mind of her own, his own, can follow me, can become a leader, can become a vessel of love, can become a bright Light. Otherwise, the dependence of their thinking upon the opinions of others is too limiting.

Anyone who accepts the limitations of what he has been taught, cannot follow in my footsteps. He can perhaps in his own simple way love me and be my friend, and he can accept my grace. You don't have to be my follower to accept my offer of grace. But, accepting my offer of grace does not mean you will truly follow in my footsteps, for there is leadership and wisdom as well as loyalty. There are people who believe themselves, in all honesty, to be committed to me and they are, in the sense that a sheep is committed to the flock of a shepherd. But, I didn't call you to follow me in the sense of the shepherd, saying, "Come along now, sheep, and follow me." I called you as a being of God's own Light to become a shepherd, as I am.

To follow in my footsteps is to step into the footsteps of Godhood. So, someone who honors the teachings of his parents, someone who is so humanly bonded to his human family that he cannot turn his back on brother and sister, cannot truly follow me.

There's one more point I would like to make that relates to this passage. If I should say to you, "I'm going to give you a gift, and I'm going to let you choose which of two options you may have for this gift. I will either give you a slave who will do your bidding in everything, who will bow down before you and kiss your feet, and you will own this slave completely, or if you prefer, I will give you a companion to walk beside you. The companion will not bow down and kiss your feet. There will be times when your companion will have an opinion that does not entirely agree with yours, and may even argue with you about this. The companion will walk beside you instead of a few paces behind, and will be your equal instead of your inferior. I ask you, which one would you rather have?"

Most people would choose the companion. And so, now I say to you, when I am offered the same choice, what makes you think I'd rather have the slave? What makes you think I would rather be worshipped than valued for who I am? What makes you think I have no tolerance for someone who is willing to speak his or her mind, even if he or she doesn't always agree with me? What makes you think I want a 'yes' man and nothing more?

I would rather see you learn and grow and become my companion to walk beside me. For, your value then to me, in my perception, is greater than it was when you were only a naïve child, expected and expecting to do the bidding of your elders. I would rather see you grow up and be my friend – even if you give me a hard time!

What about the person who would truly choose the slave? We can say he is grounded in power-over based thinking, so that only by taking someone else's power does he perceive himself to be growing in power and therefore, greater. I don't need a slave to tell me who I am! I don't need a slave to remind me that I am powerful! I know who I am.

I don't want someone to slavishly follow me. I want a free thinker. And, if you are slavishly following the teachings of your traditions, then you cannot truly follow me. Come. Follow in my footsteps and become a leader like me. Have I not said that everything I do, this you will do and more?

Passage 56

Jesus said, "He who has known the world has found a corpse, and he who has found a corpse, the world is not worthy of him."

He who has known the world, in this instance, known the world as opposed to known God, he who has experienced the world and worldly things, has only fallen upon a corpse. Here the word corpse means corporeal, embodied, illusionary; it is maya. It is the corpus, the physical manifestation.

He who has discovered that it is only a corpse, only a body, only maya, of him, the world is not worthy. He who has discovered the meaning of worldliness, will no longer be dominated by it. Those who are dominated by maya don't understand that it is maya. It is not pure energy. It is illusionary manifestation.

He who has discovered that, of him the world is not worthy. Of him, the world is not enough, and for him the world is not enough. The illusionary world can no longer contain him, for he knows there is more. Think of some people who have worldly wealth, who look at what they have and look at the world in which they live, the physical embodiments in which they live, and they say, "I understand that all of this is worldliness. It is materialism, and it is not enough for me. It is not enough to satisfy my heart and soul."

We can use King Midas as the example. King Midas prayed to the heavens, to the Gods, to give him the golden touch, so that everything he touched would turn to gold. In other words, he was very much invested in the perception of the value in the material, the corpus of the world. So, a wise and benevolent God reached down and said, "Be careful what you ask for. You might get it." And, the wise God bestowed upon King Midas exactly what he asked for; the golden touch.

So, when he wanted to eat an apple, he touched the apple and it turned to gold. And, when he wanted to drink a flagon of beer, he took the flagon, it turned to gold and he was pleased. But, as soon as the beer touched his lips, it, too, turned to gold. Then, of course, the worst was when his little daughter, whom he loved, ran toward him, and even though he tried to warn her away, she hugged him and was turned into a golden statue. In his great remorse he said, "I get it! I see the difference between material wealth and value. They are not the same thing as I once believed." And, he prayed, not for his own sake, but for hers. He prayed to have the golden touch taken away – and all his wealth, because then he didn't care for it any longer. When he was laid low materially and made poor, he was a happy man in his heart. Instant karma.

You see, in the Kabalah, there is a point where the creative force is vested in what we call man, which is the higher self of humanity. The creative force shapes the maya, shapes the illusion, shapes the material world, and then, begins to identify with his own creation. And, instead of saying, "I made this wonderful world," he says, "I *am* this creature I have made," and identifies with the material world. The problem is when he forgets that he is more than a corpse, a corpus, and forgets the enlightening force within the body that creates the living experiential being. For, there is no experience without perception, without consciousness, and the Light within is that consciousness in humanity.

Passage 57

Jesus said, "The Kingdom of the Father is like a man who had (good) seed. His enemy came by night, he sowed a weed among the good seed. The man did not let them pull up the weed. He said to them, 'Lest you go and pull up the weed and you pull up the wheat with it.' For on the day of the harvest the weeds will appear; they will pull them up and burn them."

God did indeed sow good seed upon this earth. And, then there were those who came and threw in some weed seed. So, someone went to God and said, "There are some mischief-makers running around throwing weed seed into your fine field. Let's flame it, and pull up the weeds at least." And God said, "Let's see how they grow up, for you know those little weed seedlings are sometimes hard to distinguish from the good seedlings because they have not yet matured; they have not shown their true colors. Their character has not made itself apparent. When they have grown up, it will be easy enough to tell the difference between the good ones and the weeds. We can pull them up, then, and discard them."

The fact that it was all part of the duality plan, would have been totally incomprehensible to the people I was speaking to in my human lifetime. So, I made no real reference to duality as a valid concept upon which the structure of educating humanity and the planet was based. Duality here refers to good and evil, light and dark. I said, in effect, God (good) put good seed into the earth, and then the enemy (evil duality) came along and threw in some weed seed.

And, there's something else…I can't honestly say I explained it to them, then. Weeds in their own way can be very beautiful. The word 'weed'…well, it is like beauty is in the eye of the beholder. Weed is in the eye of the beholder. A medicinal plant that would be considered valuable in a forest glade could well be pulled up as a weed in a wheat field. The lack of variety is desirable in a field of wheat, but using the field as a metaphor for planet earth, it is desirable to see some variety. We can always do the differentiating later on.

The owner of the field, God, looked at it and said, "The day of reckoning has not yet come. It is too soon. Even though I know there are impurities in this field, it's not time to weed them out yet." It was a question of premature judgment. Better to allow the growth process to run its course. We can deal with the weeds later on when they are obvious and it won't be nearly as much work!

Passage 58

Jesus said, "Blessed is the man who has suffered; he has found the Life."

People who have had an easy life aren't stimulated – challenged – to learn and grow. Blessed are those who have worked hard to overcome obstacles; those who have suffered through trials and disappointments; those whose lives have been troubled by adversity. Adversity is a challenge; a stimulus toward growth – this was especially true in the early growth stages, such as those in which humanity was cast during the time in which I spoke.

Also, in those days, hard work tended to be close to life. It wasn't like today when one might work hard as a banker or stockbroker and never touch the earth. Whether one was a farmer or a huntsman or a blacksmith or a potter or a weaver or a baker, no matter what the profession in those days, every profession was part of 'life.' The abstract professions didn't have as much of a foothold in the life of the community. There were starting to be some, but for the most part, hard work in those days meant suffering through physical hard work.

Working hard, physically, did put you in touch with life. There were tangible results to your labors. There was satisfaction in hard work and discovering life. In today's context, I think the retiree who does carpentry in his spare time, gets more satisfaction than the one who plays golf! Life is more about production than it is about amusement, or simply burning time.

It is the nature of God to create. It is the nature of the human to create. Creation is productive. God, the Creator, is a hard worker...by choice.

Passage 59

Jesus said, "Look upon the Living One as long as you live, lest you die and seek to see him and you cannot see."

When I spoke of the Living One, it was always my intention to refer to God. For, God is ever-living, eternal. Look to the eternal. Look to God all your life. Be conscious of God and of your relationship to God. To look to someone is to be in relationship with him or her. So, be in relationship to God all your life. Be in relationship to God within yourself, for the Light of God is within you. As long as you are looking to that living Light, whether it is inside you or outside you, you will always find it.

But, if you die having spent your whole life in unconsciousness, not being conscious of the living Light, not being in relationship with God, then after you die, what will you have to look to? You will be in darkness, for you will not have brought with you, out of life, something that still lives.

In the days in which I lived as a human, those who carried no Light forward with them did fall into darkness and disintegrate; they went back to primordial life, back to the Oneness. But, their individual consciousness did not carry through. Back to square one, you might say.

In ancient times, we worked very hard to raise the vibration of the human so that after having lived a life, or many lives, in which there was a lack of consciousness, there would still be that spark of divine Light that could listen and learn between lifetimes. If we had taken a very early human into the Light and said, "Come, we will counsel you," he would have been too afraid. The early human slept between incarnations. And, until relatively recently, some humans, a good many, still just slept between incarnations. Even among the New Age, new spirituality seekers today, there are those who believe in reincarnation, but they do not believe in an active spiritual life between incarnations. They believe that, in between, there is sleep or there is rest. They have no vision of activity in the afterlife – the between life.

Birth and death are simply gateways to different forms of life. One form is limited, and that limited form is entered through the gateway called birth. One form is unlimited, and that form is entered into through the gateway called death.

In those times, I was trying to get the message across, that said your relationship to the Light is one your own consciousness creates, and you take it with you after death. If you have not nurtured this relationship to God, if you have not looked to the living Light during your lifetime, then you will not have that relationship to carry with you after you die. You will feel yourself to be in darkness.

150

Passage 60

(They saw) a Samaritan carrying a lamb; he was going to Judea. He said to his disciples, "Why does he carry the lamb?" They said to him, "That he may kill it and eat it." He said to them, "As long as it is alive he will not eat it, but (only) if he has killed it and it has become a corpse." They said, "Otherwise he cannot do it." He said to them, "You yourselves seek a place for yourselves in rest, lest you become a corpse and be eaten."

The lamb was being carried by the Samaritan as food. He brought his future food with him, but he couldn't eat it until he killed it. So, I was talking to them about being captured. If you rest in an unsafe place, you may be killed or captured and consumed, for there is more to being consumed than simply having one's flesh eaten after death. Among other things, we can speak of having one's life work eaten – consumed. There are those who wrote and did not leave their writings in a safe place, and the writings were consumed.

I was also saying that when you rest upon your growth path, it is then that things will come to consume you. As long as you are moving and growing, you will not be set upon and consumed by, in effect, the past. It is when you stop growing that you start dying. It is when you stop moving that you become static and can be set upon and consumed. The world can consume you where you stand – at whatever point along your growth path where you stop.

So, I was saying to them, "Don't be like the lamb who is going to be killed and eaten." Look to your own safety – don't be carried along. Look to your own safety and to a safe place of rest. Don't allow yourself to be consumed by the society of which you are a part.

Passage 61

Jesus said, "Two will be resting on a couch; the one will die, the one will live." Salome said, "Who are you, man? As if from the One (?) you sat on my couch and you ate from my table." Jesus said to her, "I am He Who Is, from Him Who is the Same. The things from my Father have been given to me." (Salome said,) "I am your disciple." (Jesus said to her,) "Therefore, I say, if anyone should be the same (lit., deserted) he will be filled with light, but if he is divided, he will be filled with darkness."

Well, this is a bit of a longer story. Salome was the stepdaughter of King Herod who danced before him, and she was very angry at John the Baptist because he had refused her advances. So, when Herod offered for her to "Name your reward for having danced so well before me," she asked for the head of John the Baptist on a platter. And, he gave it to her.

When Salome first saw John, she recognized him as a soulmate and offered herself to him at a level of intimate sharing that far transcended simple sexual intimacy. But, the veils were heavier upon his eyes than upon hers, and he got on his righteous, judgmental human high horse and called her a whore, and turned her away. She was very angry. But, after John 'lost his head over her,' she repented and wept. She was crushed.

Two will rest on a couch; one will die and one will live. Actually, I was thinking more of John for he did sit beside her and eat – like a lunch date while talking things over. One died and one lived. So, actually I was saying to her, as though I were a psychic, "I see two people sitting side by side in happier days. And one will die and one will live." This had a double meaning, for John will live forever, and Salome had made the kind of choices that would bring her a living death. She was already experiencing that living death by the time I spoke with her.

I was saying to her, "I see what happened. I know who you are." And I showed her my vision of it. And she said, "Who are you sir? You speak as though someone sent you. I think you know more than a stranger would." And was, in effect, wondering if I had come to hurt her or help her. She wondered if I was a dark tormentor in a subtle disguise, or if I was the person she had been praying for.

I told her that I am the One who comes from the One, for that One is whole. I have the power of God my father, and I brought it with me. She said, in effect, "Oh! I see you do. I acknowledge your power. I am your servant, your follower. I see your Light." So, I said, "You must set aside your anger and not be divided against yourself, for if you are divided and not whole, you cannot contain the Light as a vessel of Light." I offered her healing and peace.

Passage 62

Jesus said, "I tell my mysteries to those who are worthy of my mysteries. What your right (hand) will do, do not let your left (hand) know what it does."

First I must explain, if you don't know already, the right hand/left hand thing. In Arab countries, in desert countries, and in those times in particular, they couldn't go down to the supermarket and buy toilet tissue. So, it was customary to feed oneself with one hand, and wipe oneself after urination or defecation with the other hand.

One never used the same hand to do both! God knows what cursed disease would be visited upon that person! That is why people who lost one hand were outcasts from society for they had to feed themselves and wipe themselves with the same hand.

I was saying that I reveal myself to those who are worthy of receiving my revelation. I am discriminating in my choice of who to reveal myself to, just as one is discriminating in the choice of which hand to use to eat. Eating with either hand, in those days, would have been indiscriminate.

This passage about the two hands is often misunderstood. These days, it has to do with pigeonholing things. Don't let your family know what a shark you are at work. Or, don't let your Saturday activities get mixed up with your work life. Or, if you have done something less than honorable, keep it quiet. Cover it up. Conceal it. Don't carry the façade, the persona of one activity into the realm of another.

This is often applied to people who practice law in current times. They interpret the law, and they argue interpretation of the law, and they do not allow their hearts to make determinations, for they go by the law. Yet, in their own hearts they may know, for example, that they are defending a guilty person, or prosecuting an innocent one. So, it means they must separate the aspects.

Today, this passage can mean many things. But, in the time in which I spoke the words, I was talking about being discriminating in one's choices and behaviors, rather than pigeonholing aspects of life.

156

Passage 63

Jesus said, "There was a rich man who had many goods. He said, 'I will use my goods so that I will sow and reap and plant and fill my warehouses with fruit so that I will not be in need of anything.' He said this in his heart. And in that night he died. He who has ears, let him hear."

    This is about scarcity consciousness, and building up, amassing, and saving for the future, not knowing if there will *be* a future. For, one cannot know for sure whether there will be a future beyond the current moment. If I had talked to my followers about this man's legacy to his heirs, that would have been an entirely different issue. For, this man, regardless of the family he had or did not have, the man I was thinking of when I spoke, was very fearful of his own security and safety, and for the future of his comfort.

    He did not understand that his safety, his comfort, could not come from the goods he had amassed. It is an internal state of being, not a question of how much you have or don't have. Now, I am glossing over the fact that it can get uncomfortable when you have too little, but once you have enough to live on in reasonable comfort, then saving up, and saving up, and saving up even more really does you no good. If I were going to give that same example today to get the same message across, I might use a woman as an example rather than a man.

    I might say that there was once a woman who had many lovely undergarments, and yet she wore her plain old cotton panties and bras all the time, and kept the fine silk and lace in her dresser drawers, thinking she would save them for a special occasion. And, she kept buying more, until she amassed quite a collection. Then, depending on how you wanted to tell the story, I could either say that she died without ever having used them, or I could say she got too fat and they didn't fit anymore. There are lots of people who do that, you know!

It has to do with saying, "Oh, no, I won't use and enjoy that today. I will build it into something bigger, and then I'll have more enjoyment tomorrow." It is not helpful, or appropriate, for someone to spend everything and have no thought for prudent decisions of continuation of life. On the other hand, it is equally inappropriate for someone to be so overly focused on the future that they do not live for today – live in the moment. Many New Age people today would say this verse is about living in the Now.

It is about the danger of being inherently over-focused on both goods and the future enjoyment of those goods. There are people who are lost in the past. This verse is about those who get lost in the future.

Passage 64

Jesus said, "A man had guests and when he had prepared the banquet, he sent his servant to invite the guests. He went to the first; he said to him, 'My master invites you.' He said, 'Money is owed me by some merchants. They will come to me in the evening; I will go and I will give them orders. Please excuse me from the dinner.' He went to another; he said to him, 'My master invited you.' He said to him, 'I bought a house and they ask me (to come out) for a day (to close the deal). I will not have time.' He went to another; he said to him, 'My master invites you.' He said to him, 'My friend is going to marry and I will prepare a dinner; I will not be able to come. Please excuse me from the dinner.' He went to another; he said to him, 'My master invites you.' He said to him, 'I have bought a town, I go to collect the rent. I will not be able to come. Please excuse me from the dinner.' The servant returned; he said to his master, 'those who you invited asked to be excused from the dinner.' The master said to his servant, 'Go outside to the streets, bring those whom you find so that they may feast.' Buyers and merchants will not enter the places of my Father."

There are several levels of meaning here. The first is: if people are too busy or don't give it the priority when you have offered them something of value, or a kind invitation, it is appropriate to offer that same invitation, or that same item of value, to someone else who will appreciate it so it doesn't go to waste.

I was talking about how people have their own agendas, and if they don't respond to what you offer them, then offer what they have passed by to someone who will respond to it. And actually, the part about buyers and merchants not entering the place of my Father, doesn't mean they won't be admitted to heaven, except in the sense that it's true that I prepared a feast of spirit, and lots of people said, "I'm too busy. Excuse me, I can't do it." So, that level of meaning has to do with the value of accepting an opportunity even if you have something else planned.

There are a lot of people who, before I come into their lives, have something else planned! Even today, they don't stop to think, "Well, the spirit of Light may come into my life, and I must respond to it immediately, therefore I'll stay flexible." Instead, what they say is, "I've got to get this done first! I have appointments to keep." It's rather like the last passage in which the man wanted to build up more for the future; people don't really know whether there will be another invitation, or not. But, they assume there will be, and so they take the invitation for granted, and they do not honor the spirit behind it.

For every person I reach out to touch today, percentage wise, how many of them feel it, know it and accept it? Very few. And I'm not talking about fundamentalist Christians who say Jesus Christ is knocking on your door – open the door and let him in. These people put it in a context I did not intend. And yet, it is true, I am here. I have offered the feast of my Light and love to everyone, and not everyone wants to make time for it.

So, I offer it to those who will make time for it, who will appreciate it. And, they receive the benefit because they are open to receive it. I won't shun those who are not open to receive it. It won't be their last chance. It is my nature to give people another chance, but they may have to come to me next time and say, "I'd like to dine at your

160

table," because I won't endlessly chase after them and say, "Oh, please, please come."

The servant in this story didn't say to the prospective guests, "My master is in trouble and needs your help." The servant said to the prospective guests, "My master has prepared a feast and invites you to partake of it." You don't go chasing after people with one invitation after another, after another, after another. When you give an invitation, then by the way that invitation is received, you receive an indication of the value it had to the person you invited.

In the passage, the responses of the people who were invited to feast, gave the master an indication of their priorities. They said very clearly, "I have another priority." And, in consequence he said, "You have another priority, therefore, I will offer this feast to someone who will make it a priority." It is the appropriate thing to do.

Passage 65

He said, "A good man had a vineyard. He gave it to some farmers so that they would work it and he would receive its profits from them. He sent his servant so that the farmers would give him the profits of the vineyard. They seized his servant, they beat him and almost killed him. The servant went back; he told his master. His master said, 'Perhaps he did not know them.' He sent another servant. The farmers beat the other one. Then the master sent his son. He said, 'Perhaps they will respect my son.' Those farmers seized him, they killed him, since they knew he was the heir of the vineyard. He who has ears, let him hear."

First you have to realize that there was the presumption that everyone would deal in good faith. The land owner had no expectation that those who, in effect, leased the land for a share of the crop, would attempt to cheat him. When they refused to pay their share of the crop, he made excuses for them and he said, "Maybe they didn't recognize my servant. Maybe they thought this was a stranger only claiming to be my servant, and therefore they beat him and sent him away. Maybe they didn't recognize it was the legitimate agent I had sent to them." So he sent another servant who said, "Pay the money owed my master."

When the vineyard keepers, who were leasing the land, again refused to pay and beat the servant for good measure, the landowner at that point should have gotten the message. This has to do with the expense of being inappropriately forgiving – as in, forgiving too many times.

162

It also has to do with throwing good money after bad. When you have a clear indication of bad behavior – in this case the vineyard keepers – rather than just sending more messengers and hoping next time the vineyard keepers will honor your request, the appropriate action would have been to say, "I won't send anyone again alone. Certainly, I won't take a chance with my son and put him in a vulnerable position." And, yet, the landowner did exactly that.

There are those who will say to you that this verse means this is what God did – that God gave stewardship of the vineyard of earth to the earth people and then sent his messengers – the prophets – and the prophets were not honored. Instead they were abused. So, the prophets went back to God and said, "Here's what happened to us on that little mission you gave us…" Then God sent his angels, or another set of prophets, take your choice. And, once again, the vineyard keepers – that is, the people of earth – abused the messengers and refused to honor the agreement and give the homage due to God. And so at that point, once again, God said, "Well, I'll send someone they should recognize more easily, and honor. They certainly can't fail to recognize him, my son." And, when God sent his son, not only was he beaten, he was killed.

Since I was the heir of the Father, it caused the vineyard keepers to feel threatened. Yet, I did not come armed, with armsmen and might; it was their perception of my power that caused them to strike me down against the future. That is one layer of the meaning, and basically it says, "Look at what humanity is doing. Humanity will kill me as they killed the prophets my Father sent before me." There were prophets of old, and there was John the Baptist. Humanity did not honor them, nor heed them, nor pay homage to God as the prophets demanded. And, when I came, that really ticked them off! They did not hear, nor heed, nor honor with homage to Father or son. But, instead, they killed me, in effect, to try to get rid of me because I troubled the serenity of their illusion of existence.

There are many lessons that can be seen woven into the threads of this story. It has to do with patience. It says, in effect, that God's patience is infinite. Yet, unlike the landowner, God is not naïve. And, also unlike the landowner, God's son rises again.

It has to do with 'wake up and smell the coffee.' There are those who call themselves peacemakers who will read this verse and say, "That is the example of what we must do. We must show infinite patience like God did, no matter how many of us they beat and kill." It is a choice.

There are others who are righteous in their judgment who say, "There is a balance we must maintain. We must offer people a chance to pay their debts – up to a point – and, yet, there is no need for us to allow them to abuse us."

Then, of course, there are the bloodthirsty ones who never would have sent an emissary; they would have sent an army to start with. The strike first and ask questions later types. But, that is a whole different experience.

People today must decide whether they want infinite patience, or balance. There is aggressive, passive, and there is balance. Aggression did not figure into this little story. Actually, neither did balance. This is a story about being passive and paying the price for it.

In the time in which those admonitions were given – like turn the other cheek and go seventy times seven miles – there was very much a need to teach patience, to teach tolerance, to teach people to withhold the knee-jerk, immediate response of countering all violence, or all seeming violence, with immediate equal force. That teaching was very needed then. But, here we come back to the word balance. My sense is people have become more sophisticated in their striking. They know some people will turn the other cheek; it is no longer a new concept. And, there are people who take advantage of this.

The question, then, is more complex than it was at the time in which those admonitions were given. There are times when turning the other cheek is still the productive thing to do. For one thing, there are some people who, having struck you on one cheek, when you refuse to fight back and you turn the other cheek, will be shamed. The person will say, "I lost my temper and behaved inappropriately." There are also those who, when you turn the other cheek, will hit you even harder. And, as long as you keep allowing them to hit you, they will. For, when you turn the other cheek, the message they choose to get from your action is you won't fight back either because you are afraid, or because you have what they perceive to be an inappropriately peaceful attitude. You are either too weak or too foolish to fight back.

That, actually, was the message the vineyard keeper sent. His actions told the farmers that he was either too weak or too foolish to take appropriate action, once they had beaten his messengers. When he sent his son and they killed him, they said, "This person is not strong. We have killed his son but he won't do anything about it."

After saying all this, I want to make the point that times have changed, and that infinite patience is probably not as productive as it once was, for there are too many people who will take advantage of it.

So, one of the messages is that you aren't God yet. You are not yet in the position to demonstrate infinite patience, unless you are willing to bear the pain of it.

Passage 66

Jesus said, "Show me the stone which those who built rejected. It is the cornerstone."

Yes, this one is well-known and it's easy to talk about. The cornerstone is one that doesn't fit anywhere else. It has its own place of importance. So, in terms of human behavior, show me the misfit. Show me the one who doesn't fit in, and I will show you the one who is important because it is he who does something different. It is she who brings change. It is the one who does not follow the herd. Who has the capacity to change society of which he or she is a part.

If you have all followers and no leaders, you can't accomplish much. And, the leader is so often the misfit.

The building, of course, is analogous to society and the stones are analogous to individual humans. Look at all that misfits have accomplished in this world, that unusual people have done. They may be considered unusual because they are, as the politically correct phrase goes, 'uniquely-abled' (disabled in some areas), or are thought to be misfits because they have no patience for staying in a classroom doing the same thing everyone else does, or because they challenge the perceptions of the day in the society of which they are a part. Regardless of why they are misfits, it is the shakers and the movers, the misfits in society, whom others build upon.

You know, we didn't just put followers on this planet. It's absolutely true, we sent all the misfits here! That's part of what the experiment was about. You put all those different kinds of misfits in there together, stir it up real well, and see what happens! Look at the United States of America. A country of misfits. The state of Georgia was founded as a penal colony. You have religious misfits, the pilgrims. You have socio-economic misfits like the Africans who were picked up and plopped down in a strange land, and the Scots who were poor and were driven off their lands in Scotland in what was called the 'Clearances.' America is a place of an infinite variety of misfits. And, even today, immigrants are coming here who are misfits in their own countries. Actually, Australia is another good example; it was also founded as a penal colony.

If things don't change, they stay the same. Change is the only way growth can occur. Value the misfits for the roles they play in your life and in society. They are the true change-masters.

Passage 67

Jesus said, "He who knows the All, but lacks (i.e., does not know) himself, lacks everything."

I'm going to borrow some words from Edgar Cayce here, because I like the way I have heard him explain it. There are three kinds of relationships: relationship to the infinite, relationship to others, and relationship to self. If you have a knowledge, a relationship to yourself, it is relatively easy to build good relationships with others and with God.

There are people who don't know anything about their relationship to God, yet they have a perfectly good one, because their relationship to themselves is an honest and honorable one in which they have become wise. So, if you have a good relationship to yourself, you know yourself.

If you even simply begin by acknowledging that you have strengths and weaknesses, that is a kind of knowing yourself. But, if you are caught up in the illusion of who you are, rather than knowing the substance of who you are, if you have, as it would be said in modern times, begun believing your own press releases, if you have been taken in by the posturing of your own role played as though on a stage, then you won't be able to see your true self beyond the stage play.

How can you learn to see beyond the stage role? The key is self-recognition, and self-recognition is kissing kin to self-empowerment. It is, among other things, being willing to admit your flaws, and it is being willing to admit your strong points. Some people can admit their flaws very easily, but can't see their own strong points. They shortchange themselves. Other people exaggerate their good qualities, and won't admit they have any bad qualities.

Here again, it is knowledge of who you are that is important. It is the relationship to self. For you to understand the cosmos in theory, yet, have no self-knowledge, then all your cosmic understanding…well, basically it has no life, no soul. It's like scientific study of pieces rather than seeing yourself as part of the whole.

It's easy to take ego trips on the spiritual road to Godhood. You also see people manifest the inverse ego trip called, 'holier than thou,' or 'more unworthy than thou.' Finding the balance isn't always easy. And, I don't say you have to find perfect self-knowledge to understand anything else, but if you have *no* self-knowledge, you can't find any other knowledge either. If you are at least engaged in creating the relationship to self, that is a kind of self-knowledge. You are at least working on it, so to speak. But, if you are so completely unaware of the true self that you have none of it, how can you understand anything else?

Let's use another frame of reference. If someone says to you, "Here is a map of the United States. I'm going to give you 'x' number of days to get to St. Louis." You can do this. You'll have supplies for the journey and so on. You can look on the map and find St. Louis right there. But, there is one other piece of information you need. You have to know where you are now! Self-knowledge is the 'You Are Here' message. You have to know something about where you are so you will know which direction to go. Or, perhaps, self-knowledge will lead you to understand you are already there.

Passage 68

Jesus said, "Blessed are you when they hate you and persecute you, and no place will be found where you have [not] been persecuted."

Well, that's the cornerstone thing again. Actually, the way it appears in the Bible rather than the Gospel of Thomas is, "Blessed are those of you who are reviled and persecuted for my sake." You are blessed if you have enough self-assurance, self-knowledge, and are self-actualized enough to stand up for what you believe in regardless of what other people say or do.

It is about being true to yourself. The modern term is 'self-actualizing.' Having your own inner standard of behavior, of honor, of approval, and not being dependent on other people's approval or responses. It's the courage to be who you are.

You see, if you stand up for what you believe in, and after death you stand before Father, Son and Holy Spirit, explaining your life, so to speak, even if I should gently say to you, "I think you were a bit off target in your beliefs; it isn't really like that," I would also say to you, "But, I admire and affirm the courage with which you defended those beliefs, even if they were off base."

If you honestly believe, as a follower of Mother Kali, the greatest good you can do is murder the traveler, and ritually drink the blood of the traveler in honor of the Goddess, what would happen, then, when you get to the other side? Well, Mother Kali will say to you, "Though you have honored me in the way you honestly believed to be correct, that's not really what I wanted. Because you were truly sincere, I won't punish you for what you did, but there is one punishment you cannot escape, and that is repentance – rethinking – to have new understanding."

If people are deeply sincere, they get the small brownie points for sincerity even as they are losing big brownie points for judgment. They have an opportunity to learn a new way next time. But, if they knew better and did it anyway, that's a whole different situation.

The child who comes into a room, and without counseling from a parent, sees a lovely crystal vase, rushes over to it, is careless with it, and drops it to the floor where it shatters, is not actually at fault, for no one has explained to him or her that it is a fragile object. If you knock it over on the floor, it will break and be destroyed. But, the child who has been educated, and comes into the room where the crystal vase is, and willfully knocks it over and destroys it, will be punished. Children do things to find out what's going to happen next. It's how they learn.

If you believe in something strongly, very often people will test your beliefs. They will revile you. They will try to pound the square peg into the round hole. They will try to make you like everyone else because it is more comfortable for them, and they don't wish to be troubled by the thoughts that your actions might stimulate. So, the agent for catalytic change is usually reviled and persecuted, and yet, I say, "Blessed is that agent and catalyst of change, for that is a representative of God – a gift of God in the world that helps move the earth, and the population of earth, from a primitive state of mere existence to the threshold of Godhood."

Passage 69

Jesus said, "Blessed are those who they persecuted in their heart; these are they who knew the Father in truth. Blessed are those who are hungry, so that the belly of him who hungers will be filled."

That actually speaks of…well, it is still about being a catalyst for change. And, if people knew them in their hearts and thought ill of them, it is about sending harsh thoughts even if you don't do the deed. And, blessed are those who, in effect, are rejected, for very often they are the messengers of God. They bring something into the society – something into your life that, although it may be unwelcome, is still valuable.

Sometimes what the reviled one brings is a kind of clarity or insight, so that people can't pretend any longer about what is there, that they have pretended not to see in themselves, or in others, or in their society.

If there is no hunger, if there is no yearning, if there is no desire, then the status quo just sort of sits there and rots. Those who hunger, those who thirst for knowledge, those who hunger for spiritual fulfillment are indeed blessed. What I actually said was, "Blessed are those who hunger for wisdom." As they eat of the fruit of wisdom, of the fruit of knowledge and become wise, then their hungry bellies will be filled.

I have talked about healing the healers and teaching the teachers. There must be the desire, the hunger, to receive wisdom, for if there is no hunger for it, people will keep putting it off and it will never get done. They will

172

never come to the feast of wisdom. In an earlier passage, if those merchants had been truly hungry, they would have come to the feast.

Blessed are those who hunger. Who want to receive. It is yet another kind of catalyst for change. But, it is the desire for change, the desire to move from empty to full. The desire to move from unsatisfied to satisfied.

This hunger that I speak of is the spark of the divine in the human. Was it not our hunger, our desire to experience that caused us to become many as well as One? It was during the First Cause that we experienced the hunger, and from that everything changed – everything began.

It is as though upon the waters of the deep, we slept. To awaken, that is change. Change is a state of being. It is motion. It is creation. So, you might say that God is the hungriest being of all. For, it is the nature of God to create, and creation is an expression of desire – it is the fruit of desire. And from this, all hungers are met – and created, anew.

Passage 70

Jesus said, "When you beget what is in you, him whom you have, he will save you. If you do not have him in you, he whom you do not have in you will kill you."

That speaks of the God Light within. When you beget – which is to give birth to, to sire – when you allow the seed within you to be born, the seed of God's own Light, then that seed that has been in you all the time, will save you. But, if you have not the seed within you of God's own Light, the lack of that one within you will kill you.

Here, I spoke of those who were recycled rather than reborn. Today, everyone has this spark of God Light within, even if they have chosen not to recognize it or manifest it. But, there is no one on the planet today who lacks the essential spark of Godhood. They were not allowed to continue, for it was our intention that all humanity would have the chance to discover, to express the Light of God.

It has to do with the Godperson within. That was a hard thing for me to try to explain to people. The inner being – the being of God within you – if you have it, it will save you. It will illuminate you now and forever.

People had to develop that spark within. It was like the ember of a fire; if they didn't develop it, the fire went completely out.

Passage 71

Jesus said, "I shall destroy [this] house and no one will be able to build it [again]."

The house, of course, is well known for being a metaphor for the body. But, it is also a metaphor for society. It is the structure – the house is a structure. And, when I have destroyed a structure, whether it is a body, a village, or a society, I have destroyed the bones, the framework upon which it is built. I have destroyed the concepts on which it is built. And, no one can build it back exactly like it was. I will destroy this body and you can't exactly replicate it. I will destroy the body of society and no one can rebuild it the way it was. For, when I set the wheels of change in motion, nothing will ever be the same again.

The structure they might build in the future won't the same one; it will be new. You know, after my death and resurrection when I put the wheels in motion for spreading the news which eventually came to be called Christianity, it would never be the same again the way it was. Our little bonded group of rebels had a simplicity that was never to be recaptured. And, inherent in the purpose, the commission, the mission of events from which it sprang, there was the principle of change, for we were catalysts. We are catalysts. And, people who don't understand that, who try to use my messages to avoid change, are going in the wrong direction. They have totally misunderstood my message!

I was/am a primary agent of change. I am God and the nature of God is to create. And, inherent in creation, is change. Anyone who tries to use me and my teachings to avoid change is doomed to failure.

Even the resurrected body of Christ was new when I arose and reanimated that body, for the moment of transformation touched every bit of the body. It was transformed. I did not build it back the way it was. What I built, what I raised up, was new and glorious.

It is true that the structure bore a certain resemblance to what I had looked like before. It was handy and recognizable. Many times we have said that here, on our side of the veil, we don't need bodies, yet we choose to have them. We don't need houses, yet often we choose to have them. It is just something we like having around. But, one reason we choose to have bodies is for easy recognition by people who aren't yet that adept at reading the subtleties of personal energies.

You put on different clothes and they are an expression of how you feel that day. It is an expression of the activities you may undertake that day. If you put on a snowsuit, you aren't going swimming! If you go to the shopping center, you seldom – if ever – wear your house slippers and nightgown. It is an expression of agenda, of conformity to some degree, and an expression of creativity.

So, you also put on different images. And, isn't that what all life is about? God playing dress up? It's the greatest costume drama of them all.

Passage 72

[A man] s[aid] to him, "Speak to my brothers so that they shall divide my father's possessions with me." He said to him, "O man, who made me one who divides?" He turned to his disciples, he said to them, "I am not one who divides, am I?"

Basically, I was saying to the man, "It's not up to me to divide your father's property. Your father may very well have left a will. If he left a will where all children were equally remembered, and you have not gotten your share, you can go to the magistrate about it. I wasn't sent to solve your personal squabbles. I am not one who sits here dividing property."

That's sometimes what they thought. Because of my authority, they could come to me and say handle this business or deal for us. What they didn't tell you about this fellow in this passage, is that there were reasons why his brothers weren't sharing the estate with him. He did not have his father's confidence. He had not behaved in such a way as to convince his family that he would be a good steward of the property, and the property was left to the brothers who seemed most likely to care for it and respect it.

So, he was saying, "OK. If you're God, solve this problem for me. Make them give me a share." And that wasn't my job. I came to teach. I came to enlighten. I came to show the way. I didn't come to play God in the sense of offering judgment, or just doing this guy a favor that he did not deserve.

Think about how many times people come to God and say, "Make my sister be in a better relationship with me." Think about all the people who have come to this channel, saying, "I just know this fellow is my soul mate. You need to speak to his guides and tell them to make him accept that he is my soul mate." A lot of people do have the idea that this is how it works. That God will intervene on their behalf and give them what they want.

So, I was saying that a lot of people have the idea that the power of God, if they are chosen of God, or if they ask, is to be put to use for their personal purposes. And, all of human experience and thought up until that point would have reinforced this idea with them. If you are in good with God, God will give you what you want. There are people today who still operate on the same principle. They think, "If I am in good with God, God will give me what I want."

Not that, "God will give me what I need," or "God will facilitate my growth," but simply to receive what they want. The early experience of earth did support that concept. And, the experience of the Jewish people, especially, did support that idea, for as God's 'chosen people,' they had been favored with God's expression of power used against their enemies. Not only teaching them what to do and how to do it better, although that was a part of it, but direct use of power on behalf of their people, their priests, their teachers, and their leaders.

So, it was in one sense a very mundane, ordinary expectation that he had when he said, "If you're so powerful, make my brothers share the inheritance with me." And I said, "Is that what you think I came for? Did I come to preside over the division of property? Are there no magistrates for this? Is that all you think I am?" In other words, do you think I came here to tell everybody what to do, and then enforce my instructions? There are still people today who believe that is exactly how it is.

I came to unify, not to divide.

Passage 73

Jesus said, "The harvest is great, but the workers are few; but beseech the Lord to send workers to the harvest."

In those days, you didn't have harvesters or combines or farm equipment. The agrarian economy was dependent not only on the harvest itself – the fruit of the earth – but was also dependent on having enough labor to get the grain in before the weather shifted. You know, they used to harvest one person's farm at a time – it was migrant labor, if you will. And, if there was no labor, the crops rotted in the fields.

So, I was pointing out that it takes more than opportunity – the harvest being opportunity – to create success. There also has to be the gathering in of it. Acknowledging the success and then using it.

And, of course, this does relate metaphorically to teaching wisdom. While I walked the earth, the harvest was plentiful. For, wherever I stretched out my hand, there was a field of wisdom, of knowledge spread before the people. And, the laborers were few. I had but few companions. Look what has happened in the Gospel of Thomas. Thomas was one of my good 'harvesters' in the field, yet he could only do so much. There were those who came to him and they were taught. There were those who came to the students of Thomas, and they were taught. I was saying, don't pass up this wonderful opportunity to learn and grow. Don't pass up this opportunity to share high energy. And, pray that others will come. Get the word out, so other people can share it, too.

The harvest is plentiful. And, upon the earth, until recent times, that has always been the case. There have been imbalances – too many mouths to feed and too many laborers in one area, and too much grain in another. To some extent, that is still true. But, now you have a transportation system that sends the grain from the American Midwest – the breadbasket of the world – to countries where there is famine. Because of overpopulation, just in the last 100 years, really, it is no longer true that the earth is, without exception, a place of abundant harvest. But, until quite recently, the harvest was always plentiful.

You have to understand harvest on many levels. Harvest, these days, could be construed to mean the minds of those children who have the capacity to learn, but who are not being taught. They will, most assuredly, rot in the fields if they are not harvested. For, the moment of ripeness in children's minds doesn't last. If you don't reach them in that moment of opportunity, and set the pattern, it is soon too late.

Passage 74

He said, "Lord, there are many standing around the cistern, but no one in the cistern."

In those days, the cistern was the well. In many wells, it was not like in this country where you can let a bucket down and there's water there; a well had steps going down into it. Someone had to be at the bottom filling the bucket, and then it was pulled up on ropes. So, basically the passage means that everyone is hanging around waiting to do the easy part and no one is down there taking care of basics. Perhaps everyone is standing around saying, "Well, it's not my responsibility," or "I did that all day yesterday."

Now, there was more to being at the bottom of the well than just dipping water. It meant also clearing out the sand or mud that clogged it up. There was hard shoveling to do down there. Sometimes it meant cutting new steps into the well when you had to go down farther to reach the water. It's as though everybody's standing around waiting to work on the roof, and nobody has laid the foundation. Everybody wanted to take the easy part.

It has to do with getting down to the foundation of things. Doing the grassroots level hard work rather than just…well, it's like the difference between being a factory worker as compared to a paper pusher. It's like the difference between someone who produces goods, and a day trader in the stock market who just feeds off the system and doesn't add anything of value to it. You have to be willing to contribute something to the system. The well in this passage is a microcosm – a system – for the water supply. For the system of water supply to work, someone has to be at each critical part of it.

It's also about serving the all. If no one does the foundation work, then no one gets served. And, of course, a leader may come along and say, "OK, we're all going to take a turn." That is the value of leadership. Good leaders help the system operate effectively.

Passage 75

Jesus said, "Many are standing at the door, but the solitary will enter the bridal chamber."

When it says 'solitary,' it means only one. Many are standing at the door, but only one will enter the bridal chamber. A girl may have many suitors, but only one will be her bridegroom. In those days, it wouldn't have been so much because she chose him, but that her father chose him or that he paid the best price, or whatever.

It has to do with competition and success. The discussion I was having at the time with my followers, had to do with creating your own success even in the presence of competition. And, I was saying that many will be standing at the door and only one will enter.

Many are called but few are chosen. Many will petition to have their names on the ballot, but for any given office, only one will be elected. Many people will buy the tickets, and only one number will win the lottery. Many people may be standing in front of a crowded elevator, and there's only room for one to get on.

The how and why of who is chosen differs from one situation to another. Maybe that elevator that is crowded so that only one person can get on is the one that crashes. Maybe that one who enters the bridal chamber is going to the most ugly and fearsome bride that anyone could imagine. Maybe the rest who are standing around the door are saying, "Well, somebody's got to do it. Thank goodness it's not me!" It can be anything. So, you should not make assumptions.

It means, in effect, that people don't all walk the same path. Everyone has individual experiences and every experience, in effect, chooses an individual to manifest it. Even if the choosing seems random, there is always a pattern. But, you shouldn't expect everyone to participate, as a group, in what is essentially an individual experience.

Passage 76

Jesus said, "The Kingdom of the Father is like a merchant who had goods; he found a pearl. This was a prudent merchant. He gave up (i.e., sold) the goods, he bought the one pearl for himself. You also must seek for the treasure which does not perish, which abides where no moth comes near to eat, nor worm destroys."

On this one, you have to remember that in those days a merchant who had much, would have his 'treasure' largely in the form of consumable goods such as grain, animals and what have you. And, when a man was sufficiently wealthy that he could afford to put a little something by for a rainy day, then it was recommended that he invest in something nonperishable.

The pearl of great price in those days was a small, compact way to put your assets into a nonperishable form. So, in one sense – the most literal sense – that passage simply does not have the meaning today that it had at the time it was given.

But, we can speak of putting one's assets into a nonperishable form in terms of spiritual growth being the pearl of great price. For, when you grow in wisdom – pearls of wisdom, as it were – they do not perish. You may set them aside for a time, but you don't actually lose them. And, it's the only type of wealth that you can truly take with you through the death crossing. It is imperishable.

The pearl of great price, as no doubt many sermons from Christian pulpits have said, has been compared to the love of Jesus, and my gift to the world – my great gift that

186

is compact, and one who has it is inherently classed as a wealthy person. All the other goods he may have as a merchant can be lost; the moths can come and eat up his cloth, the worms can eat the grain, or a storm can come and blow off the flimsy roof, allowing the rain the come in upon the grain which is then spoiled and totally lost.

So, I was saying, "Keep your eyes upon the prize. Set your sights upon that which is truly of value." We are saying that some things that seem to be valuable and are in their own way useful, do not have lasting value. Actually, if you really want to get nit-picky about it, neither does the pearl since they dissolve in vinegar. So, the pearl could also be lost. But, to their way of thinking at the time, the pearl was a good example of a compact, easily portable, nonperishable place to put your wealth.

The whole idea of value is based on consensus reality of what is perceived to be valuable. If you are in the desert far from any watering hole, the greatest value is water. If you are drowning in a lake, the greatest value might be a life preserver or a boat.

Today, the value of pearls grows and diminishes. The value of gold grows and diminishes. So, it's all relative. But, that kind of change in the perception of value was very slow 2000 years ago. It is very swift today.

Pearls of wisdom, in today's parlance, might refer to Viktor Frankl's statement that says the only thing that cannot be taken away from me is my choice of what attitude I will hold. That is a pearl of great wisdom.

Passage 77

Jesus said, "I am the light which is above all of them, I am the All; the All came forth from me and the All reached me. Split wood, I am there; lift the stone up, you will find me there."

Well, you know, we have talked so much about Oneness. In those days, the concept of 'we are all One,' was new to them. They could understand my being the All more easily than they could even remotely consider that they, too, were part of the All.

I am the Light having coming from Light, and all Light comes from me, for I was there when we were One and only One. And, so it is even now. I am the All.

I remember everything if I choose to. I know everything about every corner of the Universe, even as it expands and replicates and multiplies imaginatively. I know it all. Yet, my focus is not necessarily on all of it at once. Recognizing the totality of my energy, is recognizing Godhood. And, as I said, even now as it was then, people are more prepared to recognize Godhood in me than in themselves.

I came as a man, bearing Godhood in the human body, to get the message across that it can be done. I was the one to show the way. But, before they could listen and truly hear me say to them, "God lives in you," they had to acknowledge and see and know that I am God. And, I remember when I spoke those words, because when I did, I let them see the Light; I let them feel the energy and there were those who were burned by it. It was something that needed to happen. They had to feel the power. And, it was a statement of power.

Split the wood, lift the stone and you will find me. It is true; I am everywhere. Not only am I in the woodchopper, I am in his axe and in the wood. Not only am I in the carrier of water, I am the bucket that contains it and I am the water, for I am the very water of life.

It is God consciousness that is an integral and necessary part of the Christ consciousness. Think about that. The Christ consciousness has a bit of a different focus. It is focused on being a teacher, a healer, and a redeemer. On growth rather than creation. It has a judgmental focus – it judges between desirable and undesirable, productive and unproductive. It would be incorrect to say the Christ consciousness is nonjudgmental; it judges but does not condemn, and embraces all creatures great and small, human or otherwise. And, yet, the Christ consciousness knows 'right from wrong.' Ultimately, in God there is no right or wrong.

Duality is only one expression of God-ness, God consciousness. The Christ consciousness exists within a duality concept mode. Christ consciousness is God presence within a duality mode.

We were many in our Oneness before duality was established. There was no negative. The ways we expressed ourselves did not carry the illusion of conflict. We simply had difference of expression. Before difference of expression, there was Oneness. The difference of expression was Second Cause. Duality did not hop in with Second Cause, but Second Cause paved the way for duality.

Remember our definition of good and evil, positive and negative. Positive is power-within based; negative is power-over based. The first evil was when someone said, "I'll make you do it my way." That was the first evil.

People misuse the term 'Christ consciousness.' It is the God-consciousness-filled sense of self-chosen mission. I am the Christ. I chose to bring the Light into the worlds, elsewhere and here. I have carried the Light in my own person into a focus and participation on many planets. It is a conduit of energy, for I could not be otherwise. But, it also has characteristics, self-chosen, of being a teacher, a healer, and a redeemer.

If you ask someone, "Tell me about Christ." That person might say, "He is the son of God." Then you might say, "Tell me about his character," and they might say, "He is perfect." Which, of course, is true. You then might say, "Tell me something about how he thinks, who he is, what characteristics make him who he is…" Well, if the person is honest as a Christian, he or she will say the first thing children are taught, "He cares."

That is an element of the Christ consciousness.

Passage 78

Jesus said, "Why did you come to the field? To see a reed shaken by the wind? And to see a [man clo]thed in soft clothes? [Behold, your] kings and your great ones are clothed in soft (clothes) and they [shall} not be able to know the truth."

This has to do with being on the firing line of life, as it were. To be out in the field as opposed to, well, these days you would say in the corner office of the corporate tower. The field rep has different experiences, knows the concerns of the people, and sees the struggles of each person in their daily lives. In that sense, I was a field rep. I came into the field to experience first hand life on earth.

So, when the disciples said, "We are living poorly," or "Things are going pretty badly," or "Look at these people; they aren't making much progress in life either economically or spiritually," I said to them, "What do you expect out here in the field? Did you come as an observer just to see what's it's like – to see the reeds shaken by the wind?" For, the people are as the reeds shaken by the winds of change, the winds of life.

I also said to them, "Did you expect to see people living in luxury in a mud wattle hut? What did you expect? This is where the human opportunity for growth is the greatest – where the need is greatest. These people are little more than animals, and in some cases, no more than animals. If you want the easy path, the luxury, look to your palaces and leaders. But, while you're there at the courts of kings and emperors, you will find they are very out of touch with the people in the field. They have become distanced, for the most part, from the harsh realities of the life of the ordinary person."

I didn't come to be a guest in the palaces of kings and emperors – a freeloader, if you will. Or, for that matter, paying my way with teaching and entertainment. I didn't come to minister to the people who had the most economically and culturally. I came to help the people in the field.

That was one of the things that set me apart and made me unpopular with the power structure of my own country, in my own times. That was one of the things that made the power structure of my own country, in my own times, antagonistic toward the forerunner John the Baptist. For, he and I talked to, associated with, taught and interacted with ordinary people. We were field agents.

If you take a good field rep in corporate America today, if she is really good, you expect her to move up to progressively higher positions of authority, and finally you expect her to aspire to that corner office in the corporate tower. But, if the field rep says to you, "Oh, no, I'm going to keep working in the field because that is what I want to do," she is viewed with suspicion. And, if she is offered a promotion and does not take it, the company will often turn against her.

I was saying to my disciples that I didn't come to play the upwardly mobile professional game. I came to work the field. If you work with me, don't expect to be able to stay on the sidelines and just watch people shaken like reeds in the wind. Don't expect to see people clothed in luxurious garments. If you want to be my disciple, you are going to have more than just a nodding acquaintance with the 'nitty-gritty' of life!

Passage 79

A woman in the crowd said to him, "Blessed is the womb which bore you and the breasts which fed you." He said to (her), "Blessed are those who have heard the Word of the Father (and) have kept it in truth. For there will be days when you will say, 'Blessed is the womb which has not conceived and the breasts that have not suckled.'"

The woman was saying to me, what a joy it must be for Mary that she has been my mother. She has been richly blessed that her body nurtured and gave birth to me. She has been richly blessed that her breasts had milk to suckle me. The woman was saying, in effect, by *my* deeds my mother is blessed. And, I was saying to her that it is not for her to be blessed by my deeds, but since she has kept the word of the Father, and has kept faith with God's law and God's loving energy, she deserves to be blessed in her own right.

The time shall come when you will say blessed is the barren womb, blessed are the breasts that have not given suck, because in times of challenge, and even in ordinary times, not everyone bears a child who will bring glory to the mother. Many children will bring sorrow to their mothers, for these children are birthed into times of sorrow. Think of the hungry people in the world today. Might not one say blessed is the womb that is barren, for she has not seen her children die. Blessed are the breasts that have not given suck, for they have not known the emptiness of no milk to feed the baby.

But, beyond this, there are also those mothers whose children have disappointed them, even if they were well born and well fed. What would you say of Hitler's mother? What would you say of Stalin's mother? What would you say of Jeffrey Dahmer's mother? You would say she would have been better off never to have had a child.

The whole message here really had to do with not evaluating a mother's state of blessedness, or lack thereof, on the basis of the behavior of a child, but rather let the mother stand on her own two feet as far as behavior goes. There are babies who have been born to unworthy mothers who nevertheless were bright and beautiful, and grew up to be worthy of honor. It doesn't mean that the mother is honored, for she doesn't really deserve credit for what they achieved. So, it has to do with not making that the criterion. Don't make the woman's child and his or her behavior the criterion of whether or not the mother is blessed. And, beyond this, do not make a barren woman feel she is cursed. For, she, too, may be more blessed than she realizes.

Passage 80

Jesus said, "He who has known the world has found the body, but he who has found the body, the world is not worthy of him."

Well, I think this one has been trod upon in translation. Let's look at it in the context of the body of humanity – the body of the population of the earth. He who has known the world, has become a worldly man, a sophisticated person, has found the body of experience, the body of understanding beyond that which one who knows not the world doesn't have access to. So, he who is sophisticated in experience and understanding and wisdom – especially wisdom – has found the body of wisdom, the body of experience.

One who has found that body of knowledge, as it were – ah, that's what's missing! It should read 'body of knowledge.' The world is unworthy of that person. Meaning he or she who has found that body of knowledge, of wisdom, is beyond the world of common, ordinary experience that most people have.

It also says that people learn from experience and observation. It takes them a while to find that body of knowledge, that body of wisdom, and step into it. Once they have stepped into it, they have no need to go back and do it again. The world becomes unworthy of them – not worth their time. So, it is, in effect, a statement of 'been there, done that.' No need to go back and repeat it. You are ready for something different rather than the same thing again.

We sometimes call this planet 'schoolhouse earth.' Think about it. How many times would you want to repeat second grade? Wouldn't you want to move on to fourth or fifth or high school or college? The second grade, then, is unworthy of you. Your skills would not be tested, your attention would not be held.

Let's relate this to earth. How much more can be learned from war? When, I wonder, will humanity acknowledge the wisdom of experience gained from war and say, "Well, been there, done that"? As long as there are wars among humanity on earth, it says the lessons have not been learned. People will keep repeating the low grade of war until they finally learn the lessons and are ready to move on.

Now, let's relate that to your life. Of which negative patterns in your life have you had enough? Remember, karma is a human concept and a teaching tool. Why keep repeating the same old patterns and lessons if you are truly ready to move on? You can either stay in second grade – or lower – forever, or you can move into increasingly higher realms of consciousness. The choice is yours.

Passage 81

Jesus said, "He who has become rich, let him become king, and he who has power, let him renounce it."

He who has become rich, let him become king. He who has achieved economic success, let him then look for another level of success. Let him be crowned king and find leadership and power. He who has found power, let him say, "I have had power. Now I'm ready to let it go, and go on to something else." Wisdom, perhaps.

It speaks of the infinity of possibilities, and that being rich is not the highest goal, nor is being king. The highest goal is beyond wealth and is beyond temporal power. And, one should continue to seek the higher levels.

Think now in terms of reincarnation. Let him who has become rich, become king. The man who has been smart enough to create wealth, or even to hold it if he inherited it, must have demonstrated some leadership skill, else he would have lost his fortune, or failed to amass one in the first place. So, in the next life, let him be born as a king. And, after he has experienced the responsibility of kingship, in the life after that, let him be born without that kind of temporal power, in a lifetime into which he can bring an impact that is not based on wealth, or political power.

Think about that which is called the 'divine right of kings.' It was believed, for a very long time, that a king was chosen of God to be king. There are people who still believe that today. And you see, there was much truth in it, for when we had someone born into a royal family, even as the son of a clan chief, we would choose a prince with leadership potential for the benefit of the clan. For, it was a part of the raising of the vibration – the education of each clan and each tribe and each nation.

Look at the disasters that have happened in human history when the prince has been unworthy of the leadership role thrust upon him – or her, in the case of a princess coming to power. And then, look at someone like Queen Elizabeth I. She was chosen of God, and had come through lifetimes that prepared her to be a strong queen.

In the world today, the principle of the 'divine right of kings' has been amended or superceded in most nations. In some cases where the royal line is intact and stays intact, you will see that each prince or princess is educated for the role, and is taught how a royal one behaves, and that royalty is, if anything, more a duty than a privilege. Only one who has been prepared can really take on that kind of a job.

So, this passage speaks of choosing different experiences of leadership over several lifetimes. By doing this, a person builds wisdom about the role of leaders, be they wealthy, royal born, or birthed from the common man.

Passage 82

Jesus said, "He who is near me is near the fire, and he who is far from me is far from the Kingdom."

Light has heat. Energy has heat, as well as light. He who is near me is warmed by the power, is warmed by the Light. And, he who is far from me, is farther from the heart of God, the All, is farther from the center, for as we know, the center is the One. The First Cause, if you will.

What I did in coming to earth, was to carry a bit of God's own fire, in my being, at a level of intensity that could not be sustained by an ordinary human. That was the extraordinary part of it, that my especially prepared body, birthed from a specially prepared human female body, carried the vibration of intense Light that, by many, is perceived as fire.

If you stare at the sun, which is light, it will burn the retina and blind you. So, people instinctively close their eyes when the light gets too bright. If you stand close to me, you are close to the fire. It will warm you, and if you can't handle it, it will burn you. And, those who stand farthest from me, are farthest from the kingdom, which is source. This also means farther from the kingdom of heaven, for you can't find the center by running away from it.

What do I mean by 'stand close to me'? I mean to align in your heart with me – not necessarily to take a stand in a public way like attending church twice a week. Attending church every week is often showmanship. You see, those who think that going to church every Sunday will buy them into heaven, are making an assumption. They are making the assumption that my fire is truly burning bright in a church – that is, in a specific location – and if they show up and pay lip service to it, that's enough. But, it isn't like that at all. There are so called churches that are very negative and very harmful, and even if they *say* they are following me, their deeds do not support the saying of it.

By their fruits ye shall know them. Nothing can be hidden.

Passage 83

Jesus said, "The images are manifest to the man, and the light in them is hidden in the image of the light of the Father. He will reveal himself and his image is hidden by his light."

This speaks of maya. It speaks of the illusion which is, after all, a clothing for the Light. A comfortable way in which the Light is clothed so that people may see it. You can't see God's Light with human eyes. Not outwardly. You have to have some veil over it, or clothing upon it. The veil is the maya; it is illusion.

That is the legacy of what the animal beginnings of the human brings, for it is that lower vibration that cannot grasp or tolerate too much Light, too much information, too much intensity. Have you ever been in the presence of someone who was a very swift speaker, and who spoke so swiftly, it gave you a headache to try to listen? Too much information for the processor, downloading too fast. They don't give you time to absorb it.

Too bright a Light is also too much information downloading, for Light carries information. You cannot have recognition of it, you cannot process it, you cannot integrate it as fast as it comes upon you. So, you have to have buffers. The images are like the buffers. The images are like the icons. The images give you just a little bit of an idea, so that you can relate to it and work with it.

The images are that which is shown to the man so that he may perceive it, and the Light in them, he does not see. The Light in them is hidden in the Light of the image of the Father.

This has to do, in part, with humanity's idea of what God is. There are many images – and metaphors – of what God is, including Ra, the sun, the light, which was one of the first images that humanity had, to relate to a power beyond and outside of oneself. So, we speak of how the Light, that is, the true essence, the intensity, the vitality of Godhood, how it is clothed in different images so that humanity may perceive it. But, even in this clothing it in images, there are layers upon layers upon layers, and as humanity's eyes become more able to see past the first layer, the first image, then they see only Light. Then pretty soon, they have another image, and when they get used to that, they see beyond that layer, and it is too much Light again. It speaks of the layers of perception and how they are used as adjustment periods.

Some people see God as an old fellow with a grey beard and grey curly hair – that is Metatron, usually, even when they call him Yahweh. It is an expression of the same being. And it goes on and on. But, it begins with primitive man – a God for me. A God for my family. A God for my tribe. A God for my clan. A God for my race. A God for my nation. A God for my language group. A God for my species. A God for my planet. A God for my solar system. A God for my galaxy. A God for my Universe. A God for my cosmos. And, ultimately, a God for All That Is.

The image of God, the picture people have of God, expands as the human understanding can accept it. God has always been the same. It is the human idea of what God is that changes. And, each of these images within the Light, in the image of the Father that is in the Light, speaks to that progression of understanding.

Passage 84

Jesus said, "When you see your likeness, you rejoice. But when you see your images which came into being before you, (which) do not die nor are manifest, how much you will bear!"

When you see your likeness, you rejoice. When you see, reflected back to you, the likeness of who you believe yourself to be, of who you think you are, you rejoice. In effect, you can say before the mirror, "Well, it really looks like me. This is how I feel I look." Then, when you see, by reason of understanding and vision, those images of who you were before you came into being, how much more joy will you bear. For, then, you will know who you are at another level.

There are some people who are growing whose self-image and idea of their likeness is quite modest compared to the truth of that which is called the higher self, or the eternal self. And, their joy will be much greater when they truly see that higher self, for they will feel the beauty of being on that path, and will share the expression of the beauty of that one, that higher self.

Yet, it must also be said that there are people whose self-image is overstated as compared to the relatively modest growth they actually have achieved. And, when they see their likeness, that is, who they think they are, they rejoice. But, when they see the truth of how far they have to go to actually achieve anything in the way of growth level, they will not bear joy. They will bear disillusionment.

So, this has to do with the joy of seeing one's likeness. When you see who you think you are – it is pleasing – as opposed to the moment when illusion falls away, and there is a profound impact of receiving the truth about yourself.

People who deceive themselves by thinking they are at a higher level, are like children playing dress up in grown-up clothes. They think they are all grown up. It will come as quite a shock to them when they, one day, must realize they are only children playing dress up.

Passage 85

Jesus said, "Adam came into existence from a great power and a great wealth, and he was not worthy of you. For, if he had been worthy, he [would] not [have tasted] death."

The first man, Adam, metaphorically speaking, had not the worth of his spiritual descendants some thousands of years later. For, if he had been pure spirit, he would not have 'died.' I could not have said to them, at that time, that the first man who received the spirit, the breath of life of our own being, was very primitive, and you've come a long way since then.

I tried to let them know that the first man was a beginning point, and I wanted them to know, in that moment, that they had grown from that modest beginning. They had not fallen from a divine Adam who was pure spirit. I told them he was human; he died. If he had been the exalted being that you sometimes try to make him out to be, he would have been immortal, which is another thing entirely!

I don't think I got that message across to them very well at all. I was trying to say, "You have come far upon the path of spiritual growth." And, at that time, they were looking at Adam as though he had been of pure spirit, and he wasn't. He was the animal – barely above animal – who received God's spirit and God's favor, and began to learn, began the path of what would be called humanity.

Passage 86

Jesus said, "[The foxes have] h[oles] and the birds have [their] nests, but the Son of Man does not have any place to lay his head and to rest."

The foxes make dens in the Earth; there are natural refuges for them. And, the birds make nests from pure instinct. But, the son of man...well, we can take that two ways. One, the Son of Man, the son of Adam, does not have a natural den for, you see, 2000 years ago humanity was past the point of living in caves as the norm, and needed to provide for himself and his family a place to lay his head to rest. In other words, you must create your own habitation.

A hole like a fox's den, or sticks in a tree like a bird's nest, is not appropriate for you. You are a more complex creature. You are more sophisticated, and you are able to use your God-given intelligence, your God-given dexterity and inventiveness to provide for yourself a habitation.

Many people, when they have looked at this passage, have thought I was referring to the Son of Man, myself, as having nowhere to lay my head. In one sense, that was true. I did on numerous occasions say to them that even the birds and fish have homes, but I have none. Not on this earth. Nor is there anywhere I can truly rest, for I do not rest as others do.

Here, the word 'rest' takes on a different connotation, for if I had had a home to go to, if I had gone to a home of friends where I was comfortable, or to Mary's home, as it were, and had slept there, still I would not have had rest as in putting everything aside. Rest is used here as a metaphor for unconsciousness, for complete relaxation at all levels, and that I did not have.

I cannot be unconscious. There are moments of joy. There are moments of contemplation. There are moments of quiet enjoyment, but there is never unconsciousness. Actually, for a God, the lack of consciousness is not all that desirable. We don't need unconsciousness. But, because I was a man as well as a God, there were times when, at least to my way of thinking at those moments, I could have used a little unconsciousness! That was the human part of me that thought, a bit wistfully, about how good it would be to be able to rest.

Here I'm talking about resting the mind, for the body was easily rested. But, to rest the mind – there is no unconsciousness for a God. The all-seeing eye. "He watching over Israel slumbers not." God is ever watchful.

How would you feel about having a God who goes to sleep when he is supposed to be looking out for you? The all-seeing, all-knowing, ever watchful God is a much more comforting protector image for humanity.

Passage 87

Jesus said, "The body is wretched which depends on a body, and the soul is wretched which depends on these two."

The body is wretched – that is, when somebody is focused and totally dependant on the physical body. And, the soul is wretched that depends on body and soul, rather than on soul alone, for the body is but a vessel, a vehicle.

Relate this to present day humanity in your own country, even among those who consider themselves to be enlightened. They go to great lengths to focus on their bodies, as though it were the body, and the care and maintenance of the body, that would get the job done spiritually and create the immortality of the body.

It is not the body. And, wretched is the soul who inhabits such a body, whose focus is upon the illusion rather than on the substance within it. It has to do with people's idea of what purity is like, what purity consists of. They are saying, in effect, if I am to be worthy of ascension, it's rather like joining the army – I must be the best I can be. Be all that I can be. And, therefore, like the army, I must go to boot camp and be conditioned. I must give up my human frailties. I must give up my human desires and not be undisciplined. They take undisciplined as meaning unworthy.

But, you see, it just isn't the same thing at all. Power isn't about subduing and subjugating the cellular tissues of the body, and yet many people who are seeking spiritual growth, spiritual self-control, think they will get it by subduing the body through mundane, third-dimensional, earthplane ways of doing it.

The Kabalah talks about mistaking your body, or the materialistic world, to be yourself. It talks about losing your divine identity by identifying with the physical. You have created this body, and then you start identifying with it and thinking you *are* the body. So, these people who are trying to have perfect bodies, have mistaken the body for the self. If they need the experience of discipline for their growth, then that is simply a choice of theirs, to have the experience of self-discipline for their growth. And, eventually, they will hopefully grow and will be ready for a new kind of growth and self-experience.

When people focus on the body as though it were the gate and the only way, they limit their focus to working on an illusion. When you, in effect, have the physical fitness aficionados 'fitter than thou, holier than thou' arrogance that says only someone with a perfect body can achieve ascension, then you have a real problem. There are people like that.

When someone says they don't believe that a perfect body is necessary for ascension, yet they want to get their body perfected to their satisfaction and take it into the next level in that condition, then that is a non-judgmental and non-arrogant and much more appropriate attitude…but it is still giving the body an importance it does not inherently have. For, the body is illusion. When these people go through the ascension process, those who are truly the purest among them, will probably go for the little Light Being form as opposed to taking their beautifully maintained bodies with them to the next level. It is all a question of balance.

Passage 88

Jesus said, "The angels and the prophets have come to you and they will give you that which is yours and you give to them what is in your hands, (and) say to yourselves, 'On which day will they come and receive what is theirs?'"

When the angels and the prophets come to give you what is yours, what will they give you? They will give you the recognition of who you are. They will give you the knowing of your own Light, for with their support, you will see yourself made whole. And, when that moment comes, what will you have to give them? Whatever is in your hands. You won't be able to say, "Well it's Raphael's birthday. Let me run down to the mall and get him something."

You won't have time to shop, for they aren't going to send you a little message that says they will be here day after tomorrow; get ready. They just show up. And, so, what will you give them? You will give them whatever you happen to have; it is your consciousness of the moment. You will give them what you feel; your love and your wonder. In some cases, people will give them shock, disbelief, fear, anger, and confusion. All that you have to give is who you are.

They will give you the recognition of who you are – not *their* recognition of who you are – but *your* recognition of who you are. So, basically the message is that you don't know when they might show up. It's like the movie *Defending Your Life*. What do you have to offer? What can you talk about that you have done? Well, let's see, even of the worst criminal they can say, "He was good to his mother." The mother of the accused murderer could say, "But he was a good boy." What that man has to give the angels is himself, his experience, his desires, his choices, his hopes and fears. His experience is a record of his choices.

Will the gift shame him? Or, will it lift him up? That depends on the person. I was trying to say to them, again, something along the lines of, "Do not delude yourself that the angels and the prophets are ignorant of what you do and who you are. Do not think you can hide your choices from them or from the Light. For, we see it all. We know it all."

It speaks of being weighed in the balance, and when you know who you are, for that is the gift the prophets and the angels bring to you, then you are the one who shall be the judge, and weigh your choices and experiences in the balance.

Passage 89

Jesus said, "Why do you wash the outside of the cup? Do you not know that he who made the inside is also he who made the outside?"

Basically, it was supposed to say, "Why wash only the outside of the cup? Don't you know the inside is important too?" This speaks to the same kind of thing as a previous passage. Why do you wash only the outside of the cup? Why do you clothe yourself in illusion? Why do you focus only on making yourself look good? Don't you know that the inside is important, too?

Don't you know that the God who created your physical form also gave you your spiritual identity? The same potter made them both. This goes back to the body-conscious people who are washing and polishing the outside of the cup, and doing nothing for the inside. These people focus on the body, but have little interest in improving the mind and spirit. It's a focus on surface illusion, rather than on the core of their being.

Think about a coffee cup that has been used for coffee so many times that it is stained on the inside. You may rinse the inside and sponge it out, but you don't try and get the stains out because you know there's going to be more coffee in it tomorrow. But, if the potter comes along who made that cup, he'll look at it and say, "Yes, this is my work; too bad she has neglected the inside of it."

Passage 90

Jesus said, "Come to me because my yoke is easy and my mastery is gentle and you will find your rest."

Basically, I was saying that you can do a lot worse than to follow my path! The way of Light, the way of Life, is a natural flow. It makes you feel good, instinctively, when you follow the right path. My yoke is easy. When you are in my service, it does not sit heavily upon you. I was saying, in effect, that service is joy, not sacrifice.

To carry the load, the burden, it is light. It is not oppression weighing you down. It is not a long laundry list of what you must not do. It is not that you must jump through hoops and observe rituals that are largely – or entirely – without meaning to you. Even now, today, in the ritual of communion, observing it simply because it was a ritual you were taught, is not actually sacramental. It is not sacred. It is only going through the motions. And, these people who say it shouldn't be wine, that it must be grape juice instead, are saying they know better than Jesus did, for I drank wine! In any case, those who just go through the motions – it's nothing to them. But, it is also burdensome to them, to remember which motions to go through. Illusions can be very heavy.

To partake of the sacrament in a communion that comes from energy sharing, heart to heart, I have promised I will be there and I am. And, it is beauty. It is not heaviness and sorrow. It is Light. Think of a priest whose heart is true. He has the obligation of taking communion every day, even if it is only himself. It is not a heavy burden; it is a joy for his heart is true and he receives the true communion – the sharing of energy in this way. And, it's not about the wafer and the wine, even. For, if he is imprisoned and they won't let him have his priestly equipment, yet in his prayers he will come to communion with me, and I will be there with him. And, it is a sharing of the Light.

Those who take up my service as though it were the yoke around the ox's neck have done exactly what I said not to. There are those who go to church every Sunday because they are afraid, if they don't, the minister will say, "Where were you last Sunday?" He is putting the heavy yoke around their necks, and that is exactly what I said not to do. Come in joy, or don't come. If the church is where you come in joy, I promise, you will find me there. But, if you come in joy to find me somewhere else, I promise you will find me there, also. It is a great sadness that, all too often, it is easier for someone to find me in the mountains and the forests than it is to find me in the pews of a church.

My yoke is easy if you are in my service. You will not bear a heavy burden. And, here, you will find rest. You will find nirvana. You will find that consciousness which surpasses unconsciousness. And, that is a peace beyond human understanding.

Passage 91

They said to him, "Tell us who you are so that we can believe in you." He said to them, "You examine the face of the heavens and the earth, and (yet) you have not known him who is in front of your face, nor do you know how to examine this time."

They said to me, "Tell us who you are, so we'll know how it is appropriate to recognize you. What do we call you? Your imminence? Your holiness? Our Lord?" They were looking for a context to put me in. You know, we've been through that before, with Moses and the burning bush. He said, "Who are you?" and God said, "I Am who I Am." So, that is the answer again. I Am who I Am. And, you have not been able to recognize me. I can't tell you who I am. You have to feel it.

If, for instance, they had been able to read energy, they would have known they were in the presence of pure Light. When I said you examine the heavens, the moon and the stars, I was saying to them that you have astrologers, observers, historians, learned men, discussion groups – they wouldn't have called it that, of course – but, you get together and talk things over. And yet, you don't see what's in front of your face. You have not been able to recognize the energy of pure Light.

When you have been at your best, I have shown you pure Light, and it has been literally beyond your ability to recognize it. So, I was also saying to them, you shouldn't have to depend on me to tell you who I am. I say often – through this channel – to not believe anything because 'I say so.' Believe it because it touches the knowing within you.

I could easily have said to my disciples, to my followers, and even to curious onlookers, "Who am I? Well, that's simple. I am God, even though I walk among you." And, it would have been true. Yet, how many unworthy persons might also be able to form and mouth the words 'I am God'? *Saying* it, is not what makes it true. *Feeling* it, is what makes it true.

I was taking them a bit to task and saying, "After all this time, you're still asking me who I am. How sad that you have not felt it." It was true that many of them were not capable of feeling at that depth, yet some of them, from time to time, did feel it. Remember some of the passages about Thomas – he was one of the most sensitive. And, John the Baptist knew it. Do you think John acknowledged me, and baptized me, and called in the Holy Spirit activation upon me because I said, "Hey John, do me a favor, would you..."? No, it was because spirit spoke within his own heart and he knew. He knew before I ever came, and he said, "Someone is coming after me, whose shoes I'm not worthy to unlace. Someone is coming after me who will carry more Light than I have been able to bring you."

Even now, I could say to you, and to all the people who are willing the hear me, "Someone is coming." Not because I didn't have it 2000 years ago to give you, but because you couldn't receive it 2000 years ago. And, so, I am come again. Not in one body, but in many. And, sometimes people look at someone in whom my energy is strongly vested, and they will say, "Who are you?"

When someone asks who I am, I could say, "I'm Mickey Mouse," and it wouldn't change who I am. Names are only labels. If they are good labels, then somehow they convey the idea, the flavor of the energy; they convey a subtlety. But, even a good name is only a label. And, even a bad name does not make the object or the person bad. It is the energy. It is the truth of who and what they are behind the label.

But you see, it wouldn't matter who I had said I was. When you have it, so to speak, you don't have to go around advertising it. It is right use of will, right use of authority, right use of, one might say, celebrity. Look today at the celebrities who use their fame and wealth to do good. There are those who at least guard their privacy, and there are those whose impact on the world is mixed at best. It is right use of power. Money is power. Fame is power. Godhood is power. And, right use of power carries with it the understanding that when you have it, you don't need to name it. You don't have to prove it to anyone, especially not even to yourself.

Passage 92

Jesus said, "Search and you will find, but those things which you asked me in those days, I did not tell you then; now I want to speak them, and you do not ask about them."

How apt! All too often, students come and ask complicated questions. Instead of learning the basics first, they will say, "Hello, spiritual teacher. What is the meaning of life and all the universe?" And, once they have studied with a teacher, they get caught up in simply walking the path. When they are finally ready for some startling, even shocking new answers, they are no longer asking the questions that would bring these forth.

People on active growth paths keep looking for the 'shockers,' even when everybody else has settled down with what they have already learned. It is a restlessness or spiritual fever, but unfortunately, a great many spiritual seekers are not restless.

My disciples, when they had settled into their perception of their relationship with me, it was rather like a constituency – they regarded me as their leader. They acknowledged me as their leader and their teacher, and yet, there came a time when they were settled into the role of students, it no longer had the shock value, the shine of the new. They became somewhat crystallized in their thinking. Each of them had formed an inner vision – his own vision, her own vision – of what was desired and expected of me. They all had their own viewpoints.

Within their own hearts and minds, they had become somewhat crystallized in how they thought of me.

Their thoughts of me had come to be shaped, in part, by their own needs; by their own hopes and fears, by their own emotions, and by their own understanding of the world. So, when they had become settled in their roles as my followers, the time came when they were no longer aggressive in asking the far-out questions.

I looked at them and I thought, "Where's that burning, off the wall, wild zeal you used to have when you first came up to me, and said you wanted to follow me? Where are those late-night, stay up all night and talk because of the sheer thrill of sharing information sessions that we used to have?" It was a sort of nostalgia for the beginning, for in the beginning, nothing was crystallized. It was all free flowing. That is one reason I had to leave them. It came to a point of diminishing returns. There had to be a dramatic change in our situation, for new life and new fluidity to be breathed into the message.

If you keep on searching you will find. People stop searching for a lot of reasons. They get saturated. They don't want to outgrow a mate who can't come with them, or because they fear that knowing too much will make them unable to go to work on Monday morning. Even the best of you, even the most restless of you, reaches a point sometimes where you say, "I can't hold anymore."

Open yourself to receive the energy, the ideas and the understanding, for you will find it. The fault is not with the teacher – I make all of it available to you. Take as much as you can. Take as much as you want. Search and you *will* find.

Passage 93

"Do not give what is holy to the dogs, because they will throw it on the dung heap. Do not throw the pearls to the pigs, lest they become…[text uncertain]."

Well, the biblical reference is 'trampled underfoot.' If there is something you treasure, you will stop to think about who to share it with. If you rush out into the street, or get on the soapbox on the corner and start shouting your beliefs, this is like throwing something holy to the dogs. The problem is that you have not prepared your audience, nor have you chosen your audience, nor have you taken any consideration of what your audience can receive.

When St. Francis preached to the birds and the animals, the words he spoke were a benediction, a blessing, and they were simply clothing for the energy that he was giving to the animals. And, the animals drew near. That is a whole different thing. But, even he was selective, and he would let them come to him; he didn't chase the animals down and hold them, or put them in cages to preach to them.

Do not throw what is holy to the dogs. Parents teach their children that if they have a toy they like, not to leave it out in the rain where the dogs will get it, and tear it up, and carry it off to some ditch somewhere. How many families do you think have had the experience of a doll or a toy truck or something, that gets dogteeth marks in it? It is virtually a universal experience! To a child's way of thinking, holy might be termed 'special.' If you place a value on a special item, learn to take care of it.

If you have something that is worth a lot – pearls here were used as the symbol of value – you don't want to be careless with it, and just throw it around. You don't leave them in the mud in the pigpen, where they will be trampled underfoot and you won't find them again. If you have something that is special to you, something that is value-able – able to hold value – then you should treat it with respect.

If, for instance, you had handful of pearls, and you didn't have anywhere safe to keep them, you would probably sell them or even give them to someone as a symbol of your love and respect. There is no blame if you should sell them or give them, or if you should find a place to keep them safe. But, to have no respect for them is folly. It is stupidity, in the sense that 'stupid' is low vibration.

Pigs don't know the pearls are valuable. Pearls mean nothing to them. And, if a child didn't know a pearl had value, you wouldn't blame the child for having tossed it down on the beach or some such. So, why give someone something that has no meaning to him or her? Why should we give our pearls of wisdom, why should we pour out our love, our ideas, our thoughts, when people don't want them? I give people just a little more, maybe, than I think they are ready for. But, I don't pour out the esoteric teaching to someone who is not able to receive it. Who doesn't understand the value of it.

How many times did I work to open their ears so they might hear, and yet, there comes a point at which my reaching out to open their ears is intrusive, invasive, and – if you will – power-over rather than power-within based. So, in a way, this statement has to do with not throwing your riches – your wisdom – away, and also that you can't force it upon others. You can't *make* the pig understand the value of pearls.

People have to get there on their own, and, to a certain degree, I can help. I can reach out. That is what the last verse is about. Seek and you will find. Ask and you will see. But, the asking and seeking is very important. Free will reigns. In addition to this, because we used dogs and pigs as the example, you must use discernment and recognize that the dog will act like a dog, and the pig will act like a pig. Recognize that. Learn to say, "Oh, that is a dog. So, what we expect from this one is dogness." And, the same for the pig.

Then translate this into modern terms. "Oh, that person is close-minded. What we will get from him is close-mindedness." "Oh, this person doesn't want to hear our ideas, our vision. Therefore, she will continue in her own way of thinking whether we pour out our loving thoughts or not."

Love is an energy, and at the ultimate level, is the truth that I love everyone. Yet, I recognize the differences between people, and I make an effort to give my love on terms *they* are able to accept and receive. Some people can only accept a small portion. How much to accept is up to you.

Passage 94

Jesus [said], "He who searches, will find...It will open to him."

This is very straightforward. He who searches will find, for I will not withhold. I will make everything available. I will make the way open for anyone who wants it.

Most people don't seek, because they aren't ready for what they may find. They don't really want it, and in some cases, they have lost that true expectation that they will receive it. Sometimes people take the wrong path, and then when they get to the end of the path and don't find what it was they thought would be there, they are disappointed. They come to a place where they say, "I've been down so many dead ends; I'm tired. I'm not going to do that again."

What you learn from a dead end, is that you were seeking in the wrong place, in the wrong way, for the wrong thing, or for the wrong reasons. Most people interpret 'to seek' or 'to search' as an external activity, yet seeking is very much an internal thing, an internal process.

A vision quest means going out into the wilderness, but what you find is yourself. Every external thing that is a part of your vision quest experience comes under the heading of a stimulus to help you find yourself. You don't even have to physically travel to a wilderness; you can do this inside yourself, for the subconscious is a type of wilderness. You explore the uncharted territory of who and what you are, by questing within. Yet, so many people don't understand that. The external-ness of a vision quest is because they need something to get them out of the rut of ordinary thinking.

There are people who think they have to sit on a beach, or dangle their feet in a mountain stream to reinforce the idea that something is different. It is to help that person get out of the ordinary. These experiences can be profound. The external circumstances give you the stimulus to internal action, internal reflection, to opening, to searching. The external vision quest creates the space that allows you to move faster into new awareness. But, remember, you're the one who needs that space created, not me. I can hit you up alongside the head with new awareness at home as easily as anywhere!

Many people don't seek, because they are truly afraid of what they might find. There are a great many people who just don't want to know. It is a lack of faith in themselves, fearing they may not be equal to any challenges that lie ahead, and it is also a lack of faith in the external source. It is a lack of awareness, a lack of faith in the evidence of things unseen. They feel no evidence of what they cannot see. Intellectually they can conceptualize what the future might hold, but are afraid to do so, for fear it will be an ugly picture – or at least, not as pleasing a picture as they want. So, ultimately, it is lack of confidence, it is fear of themselves – inferiority if you will. And, it is also fear of the ultimate disillusionment; they are afraid they will find it is all maya. Their fears in that sense are well grounded because it *is* all maya. But, they fear they can't deal with it. They fear they have an interpretation of maya that says it is something they don't want, when in fact, it is the richest gift of all, to learn what lies beyond the maya.

These fears are very much a human thing. It is the fear of nirvana. It is the fear of losing your individuality.

The fear of losing control. The fear of losing participation. The fear of losing – if you will – the choice. The fear of everything being the same and losing the wonder of diversity. But, 'sameness' is not what nirvana is all about. Nirvana is awareness of being a part of everything in the universe – a totality that changes moment to moment because the universe is constantly changing.

There are many people who don't seek, because they think the goal is something they don't want. They think at the end of the path lies this nirvana – oh, don't want that! I'll go just far enough down the path so I can enjoy being a bit more enlightened, without having my individuality swept away as the drop of water falls back into the ocean.

A big dark hole is a metaphor for people's lives. They look to the future, and it's like a big hole they can't see all the way to the bottom of, so they are afraid.

Passage 95

Jesus [said], "If you have money, do not lend it at interest, but give [to those] from whom you will not receive it (back again)."

     This has to do with not encumbering yourself with the karmic strings that come from lending, and expecting to get the money back again. You have seen instances when people have advanced others work with agreements for payment, and the people receiving the work have not paid the debt.

     This is not really so much a prohibition against making money on lending at interest, as it is a statement that refers to the strings attached, the ties and lines that bind you in a debt agreement. It is better to help someone, and let it go at that, than it is to have those strings attached and pulling at you. Especially when it is family and friends, it is better to help each other rather than to lend. Gift rather than loan. A gift is karmically cleaner. You don't want to get tied in to other peoples' stuff. And, when you lend money and they owe you money, it becomes something that stands between you and others. It brings all sorts of attitudes into play in the situation.

     In those days, lending money tended to be almost a profession in and of itself. Greedy people tended to gravitate toward the profession of moneylender. You still have it today with loan sharks and such. So, that verse was given against loan sharking, yes, but also simply against the setting up of complications and ties around lending money.

Look at the difference, today, between legitimate banks and the places that make the 'payday loans' and charge you serious interest. Look at the difference in energy. The banking system, as a whole even, comes into difficulty when it gets too greedy in the fees it charges. Credit card companies, when they get too greedy, set up situations where more people take bankruptcy. But, on the whole, the banking industry is a pretty clear-cut situation, and as long as they don't overdo it, the system, for the most part, works. This is because the karmic connectedness between the lender and borrower is more distanced and has less of a personal impact.

So, it's no longer as much an issue of personal karma, as it was in the days when I gave this advice. I was trying to teach people how not to accrue negative personal karma, and how to stay out of interpersonal complications through inappropriate money lending.

I would like to say something here on behalf of barter. In those days, most goods and services were bartered to a high degree, and money was simply a facilitating factor to make the exchange of goods and services flow more freely. Even today, although you pretty much have to do it, pure barter is the closest in terms of direct exchange. The energy of a transaction – an exchange – becomes distanced when there is a symbol substituted for the direct exchange. The exchange becomes distanced and loses energy, loses power.

I would have preferred, even then, that people could just help each other out with what was needed from time to time, and not set up a distanced system of keeping track of the exchanges. You have to have some keeping track, because some people would take advantage, and others are too generous. That is all part of the human choice system. But, the money lending profession is one of the distancing factors that has led to modern society being what it is today. There are some advantages to it, and some disadvantages as well.

Passage 96

Jesus [said], "The Kingdom of the Father is like a woman, she took a bit of leaven, she hid it in dough, she made big loaves. He who has ears let him hear."

It is the nature of yeast to rise and grow, and to support the growth of the substance into which it is placed. The kingdom of the Father, that is, the higher world, is like a woman who takes this yeast – now, you notice she knew where it was and how to get it – and hides it in the dough. She takes the yeast, and puts it in the dough knowing as the yeast colony grows, the dough will rise, and that, of course, is the desired result.

In this case, the kingdom of the Father is like the woman; the higher kingdom is the creative force that brings the leavening, the yeast, into the mix and supports growth. Think of the people who are like yeast, who are like leavening in the life of the population of the planet. These days, you don't see articles in the newspaper calling people yeast, but you do see articles that say this person is a shaker and a mover. A shaker and a mover is perhaps a modern day term for what once might have been called the leavening, the yeast of society.

The point is that it comes from the higher kingdom. The higher kingdom is like the leavening inside each person. When the conditions are right, spiritual growth happens.

Passage 97

Jesus said, "The Kingdom of the [Father] is like a woman who was carrying a jar which was full of meal. While she was walking on a distant road, the handle of the jar broke; the meal spilled out behind her onto the road. She did not know; she was not aware of the accident. After she came to her house, she put the jar down; she found it empty."

The passage is not a perfect analogy; perhaps I could have found a better one. For, when she gets home and finds the jar is empty, the woman – unlike in the higher kingdom – cannot simply wave her hand and fill it up again. So, in that sense, it is an imperfect image. It also has been mistranslated a sufficient number of times, so that only a new interpretation will give you any meaning in it.

In the higher kingdom there is abundance; there is fullness. We sometimes take it for granted, for we have poured out our abundance upon the lower worlds, not only on the earth, and we have done it unconsciously as well as consciously. Often, when we begin a project, we have no idea what it will entail. It is like a construction project where the costs just grow and grow.

But, unlike the woman in the example, we in the higher kingdom are not easily distracted; we are vigilant and watchful. So, the apt part of the metaphor has to do with how much life force is poured upon the earth. When we began our earth project, it was all so intellectual, so unemotional. And, when we saw how beautiful these special animals could become, and were beginning to become, then we just naturally, without stopping to think about it, gave them more and more and more energy. In a sense, we are still doing that. Yet, we are not empty from it, and never can be.

We have poured out the abundance of the higher kingdom just naturally; we have not measured or rationed it, we have just poured it out. And, we still do. Abundance is unlimited and ever present. The challenge is translating that abundant energy into a form that can be recognized, and used most productively in your society.

People have used this passage, even in the time of Thomas, to say that the kingdom of the Father gives unconsciously and unstintingly, and empties itself out. The concept of 'never an emptiness' was hard to explain and hard to sell in those days, because the people were accustomed to thinking that even God had limits. They couldn't envision deep pockets to the extent that they are bottomless, and that there is always more to give.

Giving comes naturally to me. There is a saying among the desert people: "I am a river unto my people." That was the concept I was trying to convey. Yet, unlike the woman's jar, I am not empty, or able to be emptied.

Passage 98

Jesus [said], "The Kingdom of the Father is like a man who wanted to kill a powerful man. He drew the sword in his house, he thrust it into the wall so that he would know if his hand would stick it through. Then he killed the powerful one."

It has to do with the testing of weapons and tools – a weapon being simply a particular kind of tool. Someone who wanted to use a sword to kill another person, would want to know if that sword is strong. So, he tested it on the wall of the house, and when he saw the sword go into the wall, he examined the hole that it had made. If it made a hole in the wall, then it would make a hole in the belly of his enemy.

Swords in those days were not always of high quality. Many of them being of lesser quality, broke easily. The warning here was not to rush out and attack your enemy with an untried sword. Make sure that what you have to strike him with will get the job done.

Now, apply that to ideas. Don't rush out and thrust your untried idea into a 'do or die' situation, so that if your idea should break like a faulty sword, it will leave you in a most uncomfortable position. One should hone one's ideas and teachings, theories and such, before putting them in a critical situation on which much might depend.

This is where age and experience have the advantage. Basically, the whole thing is to not go off half-cocked. Don't rush out there until you know what you're working with, and whether it works or not! To use a more modern metaphor: they do all sorts of lab trials and field trials when they bring out a new product, such as a new medication, or for that matter, a new toaster. They do tests to make sure it works. That was the general idea of the verse. One should do the necessary testing before just charging out into the world, not knowing whether the sword, the tool, is sound or not.

Passage 99

The disciples said to him, "Your brothers and your mother are standing outside." He said to them, "Those here who do the will of my Father, they are my brothers and mother; they will enter the Kingdom of my Father."

I was not denigrating the blood ties, but I was saying, in effect, that blood was not as important as spirit. You know this in the present day as well. Now, my mother, of course, was very special. Mary and I were/are very bonded in a relationship that is more complex than simply mother and son. It is twin souls; we are One. We were One at the moment of Second Cause.

All that aside, many people choose to incarnate into families that are unlike themselves, in order to bring an element of challenge into the lives they have projected and planned for themselves. And, when we once might have said to 'honor thy father and thy mother,' now it is a more complex way of looking at it, and I would say instead to honor those who nurture you as a parent nurtures his or her children. Honor those who share with you, as a parent shares with his or her children. Look at the simple example of adoptive parents as opposed to natural parents. If you ask which set of parents should you honor, I would say the parents who adopted you and nurtured you, raised you and taught you, and comforted you and cared for you. These are your parents.

So, I was saying to my disciples, "You are my spiritual family. There is a closeness in what we have shared that has nothing to do with whether or not we were

234

born into the same human family. You don't have to be my natural born brothers for me to know you as a brother. You don't have to be a sister born to my parents, to be my sister." Actually, it would have been a better example to use Joseph rather than Mary, for Joseph was not my father. Yet, I honored, respected, and loved him as a father.

It is true that I did not feel for him what I feel for my heavenly Father, nor could I, except in the sense that God's Light did shine in Joseph as it did in others. And, it shone very brightly in him. He was a wonderful man. Spirit spoke to him, and he heard. He listened. He honored our mutual heavenly Father and did what Spirit asked of him, which was to look after this child who was not the son of his flesh. A very difficult thing back then. And, he fathered me in terms of helping me with as much love and tenderness, as much honest consideration, as if I had been the son of his body. Never did he make me feel I was less his own, in mind and in his heart, than the children he had fathered.

And yet, having said all that, I honor and love him more as a brother in spirit than for even the father role he played to me, for he is my brother. We are one spirit, and I received the gift of love from him that a spiritual brother gives.

In your world today, there are many children who are not worthy of their parents. And, there are many parents who are not worthy of their children. I look at the parents who have been overly tested by their disrespectful, ungracious and 'wrong path' offspring. I will not say to them that you have to be loyal to your children and do everything for them. I say instead, recognize that your return for parenting won't come from them; it will come from other people who know and love you for who you are. People who are respectful and not ungrateful. People who have the same values you have, are your true children in spirit.

I look at the children who have been abused and I will not say to them, "You have to do what your abusive parents tell you." Instead I will say, "God loves you. Look to a higher level of spiritual connection to find the nurturing you need. Whether you find that spiritual connection in a kindhearted neighbor on your block, whether you find it in a social worker at school, whether you find it directly in your own heart from the God Light, do not look to those people who physically brought egg and sperm together to create a body for you. Look instead beyond the body to the spirit, and there you will find your family."

Passage 100

They showed Jesus a gold (coin) and they said to him, "Caesar's men demand taxes from us." He said to them, "Give Caesar's things to Caesar; give God's things to God, and what is mine give to me."

Actually, the full story should be that I said, "Show me the coin," and I looked at it and said, "Whose face is on it?" Of course, it was Caesar's face that was on it. I said, "Clearly this is Caesar's, so it is appropriate for him to have it. It is Caesar, who is the government, who has created the monetary system that you are benefiting from. If you didn't have any coins, any money, you couldn't be taxed. If you weren't receiving the benefits of government, or what people thought were benefits of government, they wouldn't come to you for taxes.

"It is Caesar's people who keep order - even though they show a preference for Romans - they do keep order. It is Caesar's people who provide a structure within which you live. Part of that structure is the system of monetary exchange. Therefore, it is appropriate that you support it."

I can give you a more recent example of a similar statement of principle from Mahatma Gandhi. Gandhi was asked, when he was told the British were at war, that we know you, Gandhi, are anti-war. Tell us, what shall we do? Shall we refuse in India to support this British war? Gandhi said, "It would be wrong of us – those of us who enjoy the benefits of the Empire – not to support the Empire in its time of need." And, he was right. The arguable point might have been that the Indians weren't

238

Passage 101

*"He who does not hate his [father] and his mother in my
way will not be able to be my [disciple] and he who does
[not] love his father and his mother in my way, will not be
able to be my [disciple], for my mother [according to the
flesh gave me death (conjecture: Quispel)], but [my] true
[mother] gave me life."*

Well, we need some interpretation here. The word
'hate' is meant to be indifferent to, or distanced from. One
who is not willing to distance from his family, cannot
follow my way. One who puts his family above the
spiritual family, cannot follow my way. It is a tie to blood
rather than a tie to spirit, and you cannot honor that tie to
blood above the spirit, and follow in the way of my
teaching.

Also, one who does not love his father and mother
in my way, cannot follow me. One who does not respect
them for who they are, for their gifts and talents, for their
shortcomings, and for their choices, one who does not have
a tolerance for the fact that they are humans who make
their own choices, also cannot follow my way. People who
blame their parents for everything cannot follow in my
footsteps.

Families are, by nature, either dysfunctional or
support groups. Those that are dysfunctional are working
on issues and lessons by choice. They chose to be enrolled
in that kind of a family dynamic for this lifetime. Those
that are support groups, find their dysfunction and lessons
elsewhere; they are usually no less challenged, the

challenge just comes from somewhere other than the immediate family group.

When you are born to flesh, it is a beginning of the journey to death. It is true, that in spite of all her infinite beautiful worthiness, Mary was the instrument by which I entered into a process that would take me to death. And, it is true that I had not tasted death in that way before, for I had never been fully invested as an identity in a human body. I had been present in many human lifetimes in terms of participating, of helping, of being a part of the life of a human, but I had never fully invested myself until the Jesus lifetime. So, when I was born of Mary, I entered into death. Yet, my true mother, my mother in spirit, gave me eternal life. My mother and father spirit are One. The ever-living Light of eternal Godness are mother and father; it is my source.

Anyone who is born sets out upon a journey that is widely presumed to end in death, for how many ascensions will there be, even in this age, as compared to death crossings? Even resurrection follows death. Death is part of the equation, even for resurrection. And, when the Christian prayed or said in the Nicene Creed, "I believe in the resurrection of the body and the life everlasting," this is to say that we shall live again, embodied. Well, it could be embodied as a thought form, or reincarnated, or simply putting the same body form back on by means of choice, but all that is resurrection that follows death. So, by far the greater population, when you are born, you enter into a covenant with death.

It could be said that birth is death, and death is true life. There are societies that weep at birth and rejoice at death, and there is much wisdom in this. For, at birth, one moves from an unlimited state of perfect being into a very limited condition as an infant, and even in growing and maturing has taken on the limitations of the body. But, at death, one moves from a limited condition to an unlimited state of being in which all things are not only theoretically possible, they are imminently present and known and experienced to be real. At death, one enters into the gateways of nirvana – remembering that nirvana is a beautiful thing, and not another form of limitation, as so many humans still perceive.

My real mother and father, which is pure Light, pure Spirit, gave me life. In a way, moving from the First Cause to Second Cause was like a breath, for it was in that moment of choosing to experience difference that we were born as individuals.

Passage 102

Jesus said, "Woe to them, the Pharisees, for they are like a dog lying in the food-trough of oxen, for he does not eat, nor let the oxen eat."

Well, the meaning in this is pretty obvious. God help the obstructionists, for if there is no benefit to them, yet they prevent someone else from receiving benefit, then that is just bad manners, if nothing else!

This isn't to say that obstruction doesn't have an important role to play. This is, after all, a duality planet. Barriers, by their very nature, help people develop creative ways of moving beyond them. Someone can be a barrier…well, competition is one creative way of being a barrier, as in competing for food, competing for clothes, glory, for money or many other things. You take more and the other fellow gets less. But, what I was talking about is beyond that. It is hurting someone for the sake of hurting someone. It is not just evil as a by-product of seeking greater goods/pleasure for yourself. It is evil for its own sake. Evil for the sake of hurting someone else.

Seeking greater things for yourself is not evil unto itself, it's the way in which the seeking is done that can create evil, as a by-product of personal preference. It's when the emphasis is on the personal preference, and the person doesn't care who it hurts. Stepping on and hurting others on the way up the corporate ladder is an example of this.

Evil for its own sake is a different category. It is taking pleasure in obstructing someone else, in hurting someone else. And, woe to those who make those choices, for the karmic debt they incur is heavy indeed.

Passage 103

*Jesus said, "Blessed is the man who knows in which part
(of the night) the robbers will come, so that he will rise and
gather his [...] and gird up his loins before they come
in..."*

That is very simply, as one might say in today's
language, "Forewarned is forearmed." You are fortunate
when you know what's coming so you can prepare for it.
That also means it is good to be observant, it is good to be
realistic in what you expect, it is good to be aware of any
potential danger, and if you know the moment of danger,
then you can prepare for it. You are very fortunate if you
know what's coming – most people don't.

Let's look at it from another point of view. In
modern day terms, think of a debilitating disease as the
thief that comes in the night to steal one's comfort, to steal
one's energy, to steal one's sense of well-being, and finally,
to steal one's health and longevity. Blessed is the one who
sees what's coming; he can do something about it. You
talk about a little heart attack being a wake-up call. You
talk about being health conscious, and it is the same
principle as saying 'blessed is he who knows at what hour
the thief will come.' For, if you know what to watch out
for, you can be prepared. You can get up and take evasive
action.

There are people who don't want to know what's
coming, because they know themselves to be worriers. It
doesn't really help these people to know in advance –
especially if the expected event is yet some time in the

future – because they would worry the entire time leading up to the event! It doesn't help them along the way, and the end result is basically the same. When we are working with a psychic, we read the client. There are some people that it is not a good idea for them to know what may be coming. And, then again, there are many people where it is a good idea for them to know.

If someone has so much fear and so little self-empowerment, that they accept the idea that the future is written in stone, is fated, then quite often it is better for them not to know. It depends on your 'come-from.' But, for those with the strength to face their future, it is better to know what the future may hold, so you can take part in shaping it through wise choices.

Passage 104

They said [to him], "Come let us pray today and let us fast." Jesus said, "Why? What sin have I committed, or by what (transgression) have I been conquered? But after the bridegroom has left the bridechamber, then let them fast and pray."

Prayer and fasting were often done as a penance, as they are today by people in some religions, including some denominations of Christianity. There were, and still are, nuns and friars in the Catholic denomination who pray and fast, not just for their sins, but for the sins of others. And, they do this as atonement, as though by denying themselves food, they are giving God a gift somehow.

I have never really understood why self-denial is considered a gift to God. It's important to point out that self-control is not the same as self-denial. Self-control, in appropriate circumstances, is absolutely necessary for spiritual growth. It is necessary for social function – basic, minimum social function. For example, a grown person does not drop his pants and urinate or defecate in the streets, even if he has the urge – at least not in a country where this is contrary to the customs of the people. He exercises self-control, and that is very necessary, for he will not grow and learn and rise in vibration if he is so morally weak, or so uncaring, that he does not learn to practice self-control.

Fasting as penance, and as if self-denial were a gift to God, was originally an exercise in self-control. To give thanks at a meal rather than diving right in, well, it's not fasting, but it is self-control. To use knives, forks and spoons instead of fingers and fangs, is also self-control. But, fasting is a way of saying, "Ah. I have developed progressively higher levels of self-control." As a demonstration of self-control, it is quite effective, and yet, it is passé and was largely passé already, as a means of demonstrating self-control, in the days in which I spoke.

It was good exercise in another sense for them, because it demonstrated to them that in times of scarcity of food, they would not die easily from not eating. Therefore, the occasional fasting was not that bad an idea. It was then, as it is now, a genuine bridging tool to draw them closer to their own higher selves and closer to God, and that is because fasting is hallucinogenic. Going without eating for a period of time tends to produce body anomalies such as dizziness, and then…well, it sets the mind free of the body in curious ways.

But, that is not what the disciples meant when they asked the question. When they said let's go and pray and fast, they were speaking specifically of atoning for our sins, and telling God we were sorry for the mistakes we had made. Well, basically, I was saying to them, "What mistake do you think I have made? I have no need to apologize to God for anything!" Not only that, but why should they pray and fast seeking God in a very distanced way, when God was in their very midst in the person of myself! And I said, in effect, celebrate the bridegroom, the chosen one, for the honoree of this party, so to speak, is still here with you. I am here. You can pray and fast, and go through your little meaningless rituals later, when I'm not here. For, I did consider prayer and fasting in the context in which they were using it, as a ritual with little or no meaning.

It has whatever meaning the human gives to it. God is not collecting prayers and fasting. There is no storage shed filled with prayers, and another one filled with fasting, that God stores up and counts like a miser counts his money. God rejoices when the human learns and when the human's vibration is raised, so that if prayer and fasting for an individual are genuinely tools for growth, for raising his or her vibration, then there is value in it. When it's just meaningless rituals where one's heart isn't in it, or one does it simply to impress a neighbor, God is not going to rejoice and receive those prayers and that fasting.

Remember, many times we have talked about incantations, invocations, magical words and sayings, and we have said that if you use the ritual without knowing and experiencing the meaning behind it, it will do you no good.

Passage 105

Jesus said, "He who acknowledges his father and mother, will be called the son of a harlot."

In the first place, there is a pretty fair amount of mistranslation here. It has to do with…well, if you say you are the child of John and Susan, and cling to this without also acknowledging you are the child of God, then you won't get very far in terms of what people see in you. You must bring out the Light of God that is within you, and not depend only on your physical parents. These days in upscale society, children can look to their parents for all kinds of inspiration, including for that God Light within. The child can see good – God – in the parents in many instances.

There are also many children in downscale societies – and by that I don't mean poor as in lacking in money, but poor as in lacking human values – who, if they only have what they get from their physical parents, will have nothing to speak of. There is a saying, "If our children are no better or no wiser than ourselves, then we have lived in vain." That is what a good parent says. A good parent wants the children to 'rise above.' Even in a poor country, a good parent wants the children to rise above and succeed, to have a better education, a better job, a more comfortable life, etc. But, those children who say, "This is how it was for mom and dad, it is good enough for me," won't grow, won't move beyond where their parents are. And, they will be reviled as low vibrational, low on the socioeconomic scale, or some such.

Think of children born in the ghetto. All too soon, they see the limitations of their parents, their siblings, their grandparents, their immediate society, and they learn to look within themselves for opinions. And, that is the first step. They look within themselves for the answers. One of these children may grow up to be a drug lord, easily, because he learned as a child that he could run drugs and make money and spend it on luxuries, etc. But, another of these children may grow up to be a famous surgeon, a highly competent attorney, or a Nobel prize winner, because he is looking not just at the physical genes, but he is looking at his own spiritual resources.

If you only look to the genetics – and back in those days it was even truer than it is now – and not at free will choices, at the drive to succeed, at the will to learn and know, if you only look at the genetics, you are no better than a dog. For, even a dog can rise above the genetics. And, you are no better than a harlot's son – the baby who accidentally came into being, and who is cast out and treated as if he is without value.

It is he who recognizes only his own father and mother and says "I am just a product," and does not recognize his Godly father or mother. It is one who accepts limitations. In this day and time, you could also say that it is someone who blames his parents for all his mistakes. One who says, "I am only what my parents made me," and does not take responsibility for his own choices, and also does not acknowledge or recognize the heavenly parent influence. You have to look to the Light, the God source within yourself.

Passage 106

Jesus said, "When you make the two one, you shall be Sons of Man and when you say, 'Mountain, move away,' it will move."

When you make the two as one, you shall be Sons of Man. When you set aside your differences, and bond as individuals into one unit, you become more powerful. Each of you gains something from the other, and as a unit, you can do more than you could as separate people pulling in different directions.

When the two become as one, they can get a lot more done. They can move mountains. It is the agreement and intention. You have a word for it now: synergy. It is the mutual benefit of aligning. It is more than one plus one is two; it is that one plus one equals a big ONE.

Since I was called the Son of Man, in a sense it means I was the representative of the human race. When they said, about me, here's the Son of Man, they were saying God's Light has been brought into being in a human form. He is human like us. The Son of Man, as most people would have understood it, would be the empowered vision of the best of what a person can be.

In the Kabalah, they also make a distinction between man and mankind. You know, of course, that Thomas and I were both trained in the Kabalah. Mankind is the lower self; man is the higher self. So, in that sense, Son of Man would be that mankind, the human, is truly the child of the higher self. You will be the manifestation of the higher self. This also relates to the part about two becoming one. Becoming one with the higher self.

Yet, when I spoke this passage, I was talking more about teamwork than becoming one with the higher self. The people who listened as I spoke, understood it from a teamwork perspective, in that people should resolve their differences and learn to work together.

Mountains are moved by humanity on this planet every day. They use backhoes and enormous shovels and trucks, and even dynamite and such, and behold; the mountain is moved. They build new mountains from those materials. Look at the mountains, as it were, the skyscrapers, that humanity has built from the raw materials taken from the natural earth.

When you talk about moving mountains, people have that metaphysical vision of saying to the mountain, "Yo, mountain! Up! I want you over here instead." But, it really means to create change by the force of your own choices and intentions.

Passage 107

*Jesus said, "The Kingdom is like a man, a shepherd, who
had a hundred sheep. One of them, which was the largest,
wandered off. He left the ninety-nine; he searched for the
one until he found it. After he had tired himself, he said to
the sheep, 'I love you more than the ninety-nine.'"*

    When I speak of the kingdom, I speak of the
Kingdom of the Lord, which is to say, the heavens. The
heavens don't look at the world and humanity on a
percentage basis. They don't say, "We've got ninety-nine
percent safe, never mind the other one percent." They look
at each one as an individual, and they love the individual
more than they do the numbers. It is, basically, not a bean
counter's kingdom, or a sheep counter's kingdom.
    A shepherd knows his flock; he knows every one of
them. And, not only does he count and say, "There's one
missing," he'll know *who* is missing. A mother knows her
children, and if someone is missing or hurt or dies, she
doesn't say, "That's OK. I've got plenty more kids." She
says instead, "I've lost someone dear to me. I must go and
find this person." Now, it did not say that the shepherd
abandoned the ninety-nine to go look for the one. What it
isn't telling you is that he left them in a safe place with
good care. Otherwise he would have come back, and had
to make ninety-nine more 'round the barn' type trips!
    In this instance, the shepherd found the sheep alive
and well. The sheep was just having an adventure, and had
wandered away. In another example, perhaps the sheep got
into a bramble bush and had to be extricated, and that is

how this passage is often used. If you get yourself into a bad mess, even if you made some missteps that got you in the mess, I will come after you and help you find a way out. You may be scratched, you may have learned some hard lessons – or not have learned – but I will come after you to help you because I am, in that sense, the good shepherd and I care for all of you. I love you enough to go after you.

The part about loving "more than the ninety-nine," simply means the shepherd loved that sheep enough to leave the others to search for it. The shepherd did not forsake the others – that was never my intended meaning. I would have done the same, and said the same, for any sheep in my flock.

Humans have needed that shepherd God image from the very beginning. It is a deep human need to know, to feel, that there is someone or something stronger, wiser, more powerful than the self. When the child no longer has mother and father to cling to, can on longer say, "Tell me what to do and protect me," then he or she looks to a surrogate parent at a higher level. That is the first, the primary concept of Godhood. A God will help me like a good parent.

There are many passages in the Bible, especially in the New Testament, that speak of God's love for man and for the individual human, for not a single sparrow falls to earth without God knowing it. And, if God knows every sparrow, then think God also knows every human, for the mind of God is infinite and encompasses All.

truly enjoying the benefit of the Empire, but at that time, from a particular political point of view, it was a valid statement.

One could also argue that the Hebrews weren't really enjoying the Roman Empire, and yet, from the political point of view, it could be argued that it was appropriate for them to support it. When you are within a system, you must work within that system. Here you are, today, within a governmental system, and I will not say refuse to pay your taxes, don't submit to the government, and refuse to do what is required by law. I won't say do this, and claim you are doing it the name of a higher law, because you are in the system. Yet, there is a higher system and a higher law. And, with regard to spiritual matters, with regard to that higher system, keep that higher law and return to Spirit what is appropriately returned to Spirit.

Give God what belongs to God. Your very life belongs to God. Your love, your intelligence, your physical body, everything belongs to God. And, because I am God, I partake of that which is God's. Give your love to God, for that is the coin of God's kingdom.

Give your desire to learn to God, for that is pleasing to God. Be open. Be aware. And, sometimes the greatest thing you can give to God is to accept God's gifts without quibbling about it; just accept them.

Passage 108

Jesus said, "He who drinks from my mouth will be as I am, and I will be he, and the things that are hidden will be revealed to him."

This is the same kind of statement that you may find in Genesis, when it speaks of God breathing the breath of life into the human creature, and into all creatures. To drink from my mouth, to receive the spirit from me, has several layers of meaning.

One is to receive the energy of my breath and we become as one. And, when you receive this energy, there is more to it than just being exposed to it; receiving means taking it in and using it. To drink from my mouth also means, that when you hear my words and receive the thoughts that are contained in my words, then we come to a mutual understanding in which we are so harmoniously attuned one to another, that we can read each other's mind and nothing is hidden.

Also, in that time in which I spoke, to say "drink from my mouth," was simply more politically correct than saying "drink from my hands." Although, I might have said, "Receive from my hands the water of life." Energy flows like water, and for people who did not have the word connotation 'energy' in which to clothe the concept of the flow, water was what they used as a metaphor.

So, you look at the different layers of meaning. Think of the romantic kiss. It is an intimate sharing, and not just as someone modern put it, 'swapping germs.' It is an acceptance of what the other person has to offer, and a sharing of what you have to give. It is an acceptance of the energy, an acceptance of the chemical exchange. It is the acceptance of a moment of harmony.

Sharing at that level, you have no secrets. You couldn't keep secrets from one another, but it would also be inappropriate to try. When you really love someone, you tell that person how you feel. You communicate. Look at modern day love relationships. Look at how many people say, "He doesn't communicate," or "She doesn't tell me how she feels," or "It isn't working for me because there is no intimacy in our communication."

There are people you withhold from, for you do not choose to become one at that level. You see, ultimately, the only way two humans can truly be as one, is if we – guides, angels, figures of faith – are a part of it, too. And, that is what was intended when we talked about God being present in every act of intimacy and sharing. If God is not present, it can't be a complete sharing. It is only an animal exchange.

That is true of all relationships, not just socio-sexual ones. Think of mother and child. If God is not present in the mother, then there is not an intimate relationship with the child. If God is not present in the child, there is no intimate relationship with the mother. There is only an illusion, and the illusion is put in place, and held in place by society and the expectations of the culture.

In another example, people who work for a company are economically in a position of having, or failing to have, an intimate relationship. And, if God is not a part of it, if the employee is not good – as in Godly – and has not the intention to enter into a Godly relationship, in which honor and truth and honest exchange are a part of it, then there is no relationship. In the same way, if those in authority in the company are not Godly in their intent, then they are not truly in an intimate relationship with those

256

under their authority and control. And, where that is the case, the economic venture will fail.

You can weed out the bottom layers, but you can't weed out from the top. And, where there is no spiritual presence in those who create a company, it will fail. It is a recognition of vibration, and remember we have talked about how a leadership role is to lift up the vibration of those who are the followers, if you will. A good leader trains the leaders of the future. A good leader nurtures and nourishes even the least of his or her followers. Even if a leader has ninety and nine who are making it just fine, the leader will look at the one, and wonder what can be done to correct the situation that is clearly not working.

Passage 109

Jesus said, "The Kingdom is like a man who had a treasure [hidden] in his field, and he did not know it. And [after] he died, he left it to his son. His son did not know, he received the field, he sold [it] and he who bought it, he went, while he was plowing, [he found] the treasure. He began to lend money at interest to [whom] he wished."

The kingdom - the earth, humanity – is like a man who had a field with a treasure in it, and did not know it. He passed on what he had to give to his son, and his son also didn't 'find' the treasure. And, the son sold the field, as in, he gave away that which he did not know he had, in exchange for money. If you think about it, humanity had a treasure within itself, within its field of knowledge, its field of being-ness, and did not know it. Me.

It's not knowing – or recognizing – what you have until it is too late. Many people don't understand their honor, so they have sold it or given it away. And, it's only then that they say, "I have let go of something that was important to me." Many people don't understand the treasure of their talents until they have sold them, or given them away, and someone else is making money off of them.

It is also selling what you have without understanding it, and without honoring its continuity. You see, in the days in which I spoke, to sell the field, unless the son was childless, was an irresponsible act. It would deprive future generations of his family of their patrimony, possibly even their livelihood. To sell the family farm, unless urban renewal has forced you into it, or unless your children have all gone off voluntarily to work in factories and you need the money to live on in your old age, is not honoring the continuity, the needs of the future. In any case, the field is a legacy. A man had a legacy from his father and from his heavenly Father, and there was a treasure in the field, the legacy, that he did not recognize.

His son, in a similar way, didn't dig deep enough to find it, and didn't value it all that much. But, a prospective buyer came along and recognized the value. Now, in the context of the story, he may not have known there was a treasure in it; it may have been the treasure was not buried gold or coin, but the treasure could have been the level of fertility that a carefully managed field would have brought forth.

The ability to produce a richer harvest is really what we're talking about here. Whether it is done by increasing the productivity of a field where its fertility has not been fully explored, whether it is in the metaphor of finding buried treasure, whether it is finding the unrecognized treasure within one's self, it's still about unrecognized value. And, the one who recognizes the value and puts out the money to buy it, or does the work to obtain it, is the one who gets the reward.

The buried treasure is simply a metaphor for unrecognized value, wherever it is found. The one who recognizes the value, who finds it, is the one who will reap the profits. And, that is as it should be.

Passage 110

Jesus said, "He who has found the world and becomes rich, let him deny the world."

He who has learned what there is to learn from his community and his extended community, and has profited from it, he who has become wealthy…well, in your society you have people who say, "Been there. Done that. Now what?" One who has succeeded, as far as creating wealth goes, if he or she is a balanced person, won't continue to get more and more and more wealth accumulated, just for the sake of being able to count into the higher numbers. Instead, the person will look for something else to do.

Many people today will say to you, "I left a successful career as thus-and-so, because I wanted to get more out of life." So, it is a question of shifting values. When someone has what they consider to be enough money, or even more than enough money, then the completion that flows from this will often create a shift of values.

If someone has 'been there, done that,' it becomes a shift to a higher purpose. It's a type of denying the world. In other words, the person who becomes rich, or is born into wealth, does not allow the wealth to rule them. They do not make decisions based on fear of loss, or on seeking to gain monetarily. In effect, a balanced person will say, "I have enough." They acknowledge having enough for their own needs, enough to pass on to any children, and enough to share. So, one who 'denies' the world, simply moves to the next higher level in which 'worldliness,' or lower chakra vibrations, no longer dominate. Of course, you don't have to be wealthy to deny the world.

To deny the world is to move your focus, your energy, even up to and including what you have received from the earth, to a higher level of wisdom and understanding, a higher level of experience, a higher level of seeking. And, to do that, you must deny the world. You cannot let it hold you back. You cannot let it make your choices for you. You cannot let it dictate to you.

If the world says "frog," and you are still jumping every time, then you have not denied the earth. But, if the world says "frog," and you don't jump, you have denied the world, have you not? The world today, the society in which you live, is denied in many ways, small as well as great, by people who have come to a place of wealth within themselves, which may or may not have anything to do with money.

The people who go and live in the woods, and build their own cabins with their own hands, are denying the world and searching for something higher. Something more powerful, more beautiful, more fulfilling than what they received from the urban society of which they otherwise were a part. That is not the same thing as the apocalyptic paranoid class who builds bunkers, and takes everything with them against the presumed day of need; that is different. If you stop and think about it, that is jumping when the world says "frog."

Passage 111

Jesus said, "The heavens and the earth will roll back in your presence, and he who lives by the Living One will not see death not…" because Jesus said, "He who finds himself, the world is not worthy of him."

So many times they asked me, "Tell us about yourself. But, really…who you are, how you feel, what must it be like to be you." It was very hard to answer, for they had no context on which to base an understanding of who and what I was. And, I would say to myself, "What can I tell them? What can I say to them that will have meaning to them, about who I am? How can I speak in metaphors and images they will understand?"

So, I said, "Heaven and earth will roll back before your eyes. The barriers – the clouds – between earth and heaven, the veils that prevented you from seeing God, have been pushed aside that you might see me and know me." And, in their presence, God had rolled back the heavens and earth, and created an energy form into which the Light could be contained, and I am He.

The enormity of the task we undertook, was to contain true Godhood, very God of very God, very Light of very Light, in the form of a human body. And not just contain it in a form, but into the working parts of the human body, put the pure Light of God. What an undertaking!

In spite of the fact that I am one with All, it is also true to say that I didn't do it alone. There were many who had roles to play, and each of us played his or her role as

262

best we could, and as best thought. And, to explain this to them, it was very hard to find the words.

Blessed is he who finds himself, for the world is not worthy of him. You know, even I in all my power, and in all my knowing of who I was – which I did know from the beginning – in the human side of it, in a way, I had to find myself. You can know yourself without having found yourself experientially. You can know intellectually who you are, but to live it, to *be* the living Light, was something else entirely.

To know who you are, and then to experience the fullness of who you are, are two different things. Knowing it intellectually, and knowing it by experience, are two different things. It's hard to say when exactly I came to the place of living it, being the living Light, fully conscious of it, fully focused on it all the time. I didn't fully focus on it in the beginning. In the beginning, I focused on my humanity, and yet the time came when I was living it. I was the living Light, and the more I was the living Light, the more I was separated from those around me – even those I loved most. And, the more powerful I became as I lived the Light, the more I knew the time would come when I must move into the next dimension.

What would the people around me have said or done, what would their fears have been if they had looked down at my feet, and found they weren't touching the ground? Do you know how much trouble it was to keep my feet on the ground? They would have been terrified, and would have run away, and some of them would have called me devil. Just as might happen today. In any case, I had to keep my feet on the ground if only to prove that I was human. Had Michael walked above the ground, they would have said, "Oh, it's an angel."

People fear a power higher than themselves. They fear it is either God coming to punish them, or the Devil trying to find a way to hurt them. People fear power instinctively. Look at the primitive pre-human creature when lightening started a fire in the forest. Of course he feared the fire, why wouldn't he? And later, when he could kindle fire and keep the coals alive, still he knew it could hurt him.

The part about worth has to do with recognition of value. When we speak of pearls or jewelry, we speak of the cultural perception of what worth is. But, when you speak of the Light, there's more to it than just cultural perception, for if the Light is upon you and you do not feel it, if it is before you and you do not see it, if it has been offered to you and you have not the sense to take it, then you are unworthy of it.

One who has come to know himself as the living Light, of him, the world is not worthy. The world cannot receive his value for the world cannot comprehend it.

Passage 112

*Jesus said, "Woe to the flesh which depends on the soul;
woe to the soul which depends on the flesh."*

Woe to the flesh that depends on the soul to do everything for it. Woe to the soul that expects the flesh to get the job done. Well, sometimes I repeated myself, and sometimes other people repeated their favorite sayings or stories!

In a curious way, this is also like saying, "Don't send a boy to do a man's job." It means that both soul and flesh have their roles to play in the integration of what we call the human being – both animal and Godly. You don't expect the soul to do such flesh tasks as sleep, eat, bathing, pull the splinter out of your foot, or go to the bathroom; these are activities associated with the body, the flesh.

Yet, woe to the soul that depends upon the flesh. Woe to soul that is so captivated by the illusion of flesh, that it has forgotten soul-ness. I refer again to Kabbalistic teaching. Man, the higher self, created mankind, or what we call humanity, and then he began to identify with what he had created. Mankind also creates ideas, imaginative situations, circumstances, opportunities for decisions, lessons, diversity, art – all manner of things. He then begins to identify the object he has created with the body. And, the balance is lost when all the focus is directed to the body.

A perfect body will not create a perfect soul. It is also true that the soul may not create a perfect body. And, a perfect soul still, in effect, has to pay attention to the body occasionally, if it wants to remain incarnate and functional.

There is a certain amount of respect that should be given to the body. There is this vision that some people have of a spiritual ascetic, like the guru on the mountaintop where his hair and beard are long and unkempt, his fingers and toenails have grown claw-like, and he is unwashed. I do not find such an unwashed, unkempt, untidy creature, who is so totally disrespectful of his body, to be inherently, by reason of those particular choices, spiritual.

The body's needs should be respected and attended to in appropriate ways. Even those people – and this goes back to that passage about prayer and fasting and penance – who for instance say, "Well, I'm too spiritual to feel any interest in sex. I'm too spiritual to have an appetite." That is a denial of the body; it is a self-denial of the physical. I think it is preferable to have balance, rather than denial of the body.

God did not create the body full of pitfalls and traps. There is nothing about the human body that is – or was – entirely without purpose. Now, you can argue that the appendix is no longer needed, and I would agree. The body has evolved. In any case, in creating the human body in the way in which human bodies were created, God wasn't setting traps for humanity. God, in effect, set up a working machine – very elegant and complex. I think it is a lovely creation, especially in all its diversity.

By the same token, no matter how beautiful that body is that God has created, without a soul, it is of no more light or life than a statue. Humanity, to start with, was illuminated by the Light of the Maker, for the Maker desired to see 'real' life rather than just statues.

266

Passage 113

His disciples said to him, "On what day will the Kingdom come?" (He said,) "It will not come by expectation. They will not say, 'Look here,' but the Kingdom of the Father is spread out on the earth and men do not see it."

Well, you know, humans are always looking for concrete answers. My disciples were saying, "When is all this supposed to happen? How long do I have to get ready? What must I do?" People are still asking those questions today. "When is the apocalypse? What do the prophecies of Revelation mean? What does the future hold, and on what day will it happen?"

I could not have told my disciples, "Well, you don't have to worry about it, because it will be thousands of years after you're gone!" I can just see it; that answer would have gone over like the modern day proverbial lead balloon!

They wouldn't have wanted to hear that answer. Yet, what I told them is true; the kingdom is here. The kingdom of God, the rulership of God, the creative manifestation of God, has been on this planet since before there was a planet. For, the energy of the God source is what created the heavens and the earth. It is the kingdom. It is God's territory. It always was. It always will be. And, it is everywhere. There is no 'where not' or 'is not,' for as soon as we think it, it is the kingdom.

It is God's pleasure as manifested in the diversity of the Second Cause, and all that flowed from it. It is God's pleasure that brought the earth into being and keeps it spinning. Even now, today, for it is by God's pleasure that the principle of gravitational rotation, and relationship of this planet to the other stars and heavenly bodies, was formed. The kingdom is here – now and always.

Passage 114

Simon Peter said to them, "Let Mary leave us, because women are not worthy of the Life." Jesus said, "Look, I shall guide her so that I will make her male, in order that she also may become a living spirit, being like you males. For every woman who makes herself male will enter the Kingdom of Heaven."

To understand this, you must take into consideration the image, or idea, of what a woman was that prevailed in that day and time. In that day and time, a woman was property, but also in those times, a woman was not a spiritual or intellectual being. She was rather like a dog or a cat. This is from the male point of view at the time, and in the cultural perception of that time in that area. That culture did not prevail over all the earth, but in the land of Israel and in the Middle East to a large degree, in the patriarchal cultures of the Middle East and India and China, women were lesser beings. This perception was not everywhere on the earth, but it was widespread.

In many regards, women were lesser beings in that they had not been stimulated intellectually, they had not been educated, they had not been given the opportunity to make choices, and as you know, the opportunity to make choices is fundamental in the development of growth.

So, not for Mary, but for many women of the region and the day, it is true that they were not as intelligent as their males, and they had no appreciable personal spirituality apart from doing what was expected of them. They knew the rituals, but they didn't really know the stories behind them. They only knew it was what they were supposed to do.

When I said I would make her male, it was that I would make her educated and intellectual, and give her opportunity for choices. I will introduce her to those things that create in a human the opportunity for spiritual growth. And, once she has had that opportunity and has grown spiritually, she will be as good as any man. I was using Mary as the example, of course.

If you stop and think of what gender meant in those days, people were characterized by gender, and it wasn't about the physical body gender; it was about the gender-linked traits and gender-linked roles they played, and about the gender-linked opportunities that they had. In a man's society, a woman might be recognized as unusually intelligent, just as one might admire the novelty of a talking parrot or a trained pony. It was thought to be little or no more than that.

Under some circumstances, even the touch of a woman was considered to be defiling. It comes back to vibration. With diminished access to education, to intellectual stimulation of any kind, with enforced suppression into a very narrow gender-linked role band, with diminished opportunity for making choices, over a period of time, the women *were* intellectually and spiritually inferior.

In order to remedy the situation, Peter was saying, "There's a woman in our midst. Send her away! She brings us down, brings us bad luck to have her here." And, I said to him, "I'll teach her to be your intellectual equal. I will teach her to be as wise as you are, and you will find that her vibration is as high as yours, that her spirit is no less than yours." Then I talked about going out and giving women the opportunity to learn and grow to a much higher degree than they had had before.

If you will stop and think about it, among the patriarchal societies in the Middle East – and there are many – it is the Jews whose women have become empowered. I look at that particular discussion that I had with my disciples as one of the more productive ones.

What makes a man? What makes a woman? In part, the way it was then, opportunities made the man and unmade the woman. We will make women equal to men by giving them opportunities to be equal, and by viewing them as equals.

Epilogue

From before the beginning, to beyond the end, again and again I have seen with wonder and delight creation as it unfolds in the vastness of the universe. There's never a dull moment. There is always something happening. And, because I am God, after all, it all belongs to me.

I see myself in every part of it, and all of it is a part of me. And, because it is mine, I am moved from time to time to make adjustments here and there, to share ideas, to speak to those very special creatures in whom my Light is vested – humanity. I speak to them as one human speaking to another, because I don't want to invoke the power of God to simply direct them and say, "Do this. Do that. Don't do this. Don't do that." For, it relates to the passage (#55) where I shared the story about how I would rather have a companion to walk beside me, than a slave to kiss my feet.

As a knowing God Light, a conscious manifestation of God's Light, many times I've looked around and said, "You know, my companions are few. It would be a fine thing to see some of these humans, in whom my Light is vested, and who have such potential, grow up to be companions on the path of the elite. It would be so satisfying to see them mature and step up into the companion role." I notice how very imaginative some of them are. They actually have something to offer. And, because I am eager to see them grow and learn, and step up into the companion role, from time to time, I speak to them – one or another of them – and offer a bit of advice that I hope will help them along the way.

When I was born into humanity, to establish a different kind of credibility with humans, I lived a whole lifetime in human terms of thirty-something years, during which I taught a lot, I learned a lot, and I experienced a lot. I tried to pack as much substance into my words as I could, then and there, while they were at least partially open to hearing my words. Yet, even then, I knew that their ability to be truly open to my words was limited, not by the content of my words, but by the understanding of their own hearts and minds. And, so, after all these 2000 years, it gives me pleasure that my work is remembered, and that there are still those who value and receive what I came to give.

I rejoice that my words are being restored, not only in our conversations, but also in the hearts of men and women everywhere. I rejoice that the ideas I wanted so much to share with humanity are being rediscovered, not just in religion – in churches, be they Christian or some other faith – but in the hearts and minds of humanity. For, the energy, the intent, the Light and all the information it contains; the Light is here.

And, in all these words we have shared, in all the words I spoke when I walked the earth, there is that thread, that beam of Light. Remember, information is carried on the Light. The words are like a sheath, a clothing around the energy and around the Light. You can decorate the carrier, but the core, the beam lies within it unchanged.

In any case, I have truly enjoyed this opportunity to talk about some of the old sayings and the deeper meaning I had built into them. And, I will look forward to further opportunities in the future, with you as well as with others, for as you know, I work with many people. I will look for more opportunities to share and continue my dialogue with humanity. And, remember, I don't just talk – I listen.

The energy I carry is embodied in the word God. Those who know God, know me. For, I am with God from the beginning and beyond the end.

I am the Creator and the creation.

I am the Love and I am the Light.
I Am.
And, so are you.

What's Next?

From the Rainbow Angels,
The LightSource Group
and Channel Laurel Steinhice

In that little corner of the world-beyond that we think of as 'ours', we have a very large drawing-board ... and it is loaded with information, insights and ideas we want to share with you.

We have the Cosmic equivalent of a file room full of goodies, stored in the Universal (akashic) equivalents of stone tablets, sand paintings, books and pamphlets, CDs, DVDs, Videos, hard drives, paintings, songs, self-expressions and collective consciousness patterns; the whole range of human experience --- and beyond.

Some are 'golden oldies' that you have forgotten, and we now bring them forth to remind you of what you already knew. We push the right buttons with our words and energy, and your buried memories burst forth.

Some are entirely new. We are up to our ears in new ideas, and eager to share them with you.

Some are ideas ... thoughtforms that have not yet been fully shaped; visionary proposals to consider; possibilities to explore. Or not.

In short, there's a lot we want to say, to teach, to show you.

Yes, there are other communicators who also bring forth information for your consideration and enLightenment. We respect that.

We join their ranks, bonding with them in the Light of Oneness, by sharing with you our own perspectives and insights, in our own words and infused with our own energies.

We expect to be sharing with you, shortly, our presentations on the following topics: (These are not titles, per se, but rather topics we plan to address within the next few months.)

Understanding Earthchanges
What's Next for Planet Earth?
The Nature of Good and Evil, at the Core
News on the Cloned Earth Project
Phasing Out Dis-Ease and Dysfunction
Guide to Shamanism – Adventures in
        Otherwhere
Guide to Healing the Body of Humanity
Guide to Past-Life Exploration
Guide to Planetary Past-Life Healing
Planetary Ascension
Co-Creatorship: Building Your Own
        Reality
... and so, so many others!

We also call to your attention those volumes we have already put before you, in book form:

Edgar Cayce's Self-Healing Tips (Special Collectors Edition, The Lightsource Group, 2009, by Laurel Steinhice)

The Rainbow Angels' Guide to Colors, Crystals and Healing, (The Lightsource Group, 2009, by Laurel Steinhice)

The Rainbow Angels' Guide to Exorcism for Modern Healers, by Channel Laurel Steinhice, The LightSource Group, 2009

New Titles from The LightSource Group: Books for The Mind and Soul.